# How Women Transform Preaching

# Other Books by Leonora Tubbs Tisdale

*A Sermon Workbook: Exercises in the Art and Craft of Preaching,*
co-author with Thomas H. Troeger (Abingdon Press, 2013)

*The Abingdon Women's Preaching Annual, Series 2 Year A*
(Abingdon Press, 2001)

*The Abingdon Women's Preaching Annual, Series 2 Year C*
(Abingdon Press, 2000)

*The Abingdon Women's Preaching Annual, Series 2 Year B*
(Abingdon Press, 1999)

*The Sun Still Rises: Meditations on Faith at Midlife*
(Westminster John Knox Press, 2017)

*Making Room at the Table: An Invitation to Multicultural Worship,*
co-editor with Brian K. Blount (Westminster John Knox Press, 2001)

# How Women Transform Preaching

Leonora Tubbs Tisdale

HOW WOMEN TRANSFORM PREACHING

*Copyright © 2021 by Abingdon Press*

All rights reserved.
No part of this work may be reproduced or transmitted in any form or by any means, electronic or mechanical, including photocopying and recording, or by any information storage or retrieval system, except as may be expressly permitted by the 1976 Copyright Act or in writing from the publisher. Requests for permission should be addressed to Permissions, Abingdon Press, 2222 Rosa L. Parks Boulevard, Nashville, TN 37228-1306, or permissions@abingdonpress.com.

Library of Congress Control Number: 2021935506

ISBN: 978-1-7910-1336-3

Scripture quotations unless noted otherwise are from the Common English Bible. Copyright © 2011 by the Common English Bible. All rights reserved. Used by permission. www.CommonEnglishBible.com.

Scripture quotations marked (NRSV) are taken from the New Revised Standard Version of the Bible, copyright 1989, Division of Christian Education of the National Council of the Churches of Christ in the United States of America. Used by permission. All rights reserved.

Significant portions of chapter 2 were previously published in *The International Journal of Homiletics* (Vol. 2, Issue 1). Used by permission.

The sixteen homiletical foremothers interviewed for this book have granted their permission to use quotations from their interviews.

21 22 23 24 25 26 27 28 29—10 9 8 7 6 5 4 3 2 1
MANUFACTURED IN THE UNITED STATES OF AMERICA

# More Praise for *How Women Transform Preaching*

"Leonora Tubbs Tisdale's overview of the history of three centuries of women preachers and homiletics scholars in the United States is a treasure. This is a must-read for every pastor and seminarian, every congregational leader, and every confirmand, whatever their gender identification. Tisdale draws back the curtain on a largely invisible history of courage and perseverance on the part of women who could not, and would not, stifle the liberating Word the Spirit had given them to preach. At the same time, she draws us in close to overhear her interviews with one preaching woman after another who testify to costly journeys to the pulpit, leaning into strong headwinds of resistance. This book reminds us that the Spirit will continue to put the life-giving Word of God's redemptive engagement with the world into the mouths of the officially excluded, until all are included, all set free."
—Sally A. Brown, Elizabeth M. Engle Professor of Preaching and Worship, director, Engle Institute of Preaching, Princeton Theological Seminary, Princeton, NJ

"Preaching and patriarchy have a long and troubling alliance, and Nora Tubbs Tisdale shows us why in this magnificent book. By unearthing women's stories, struggles, and strategies for facing resistance, Tisdale makes a monumental contribution to the history of preaching. Her insights are a treasure for all who are called to bear witness to heartfelt convictions. This book is incisive, riveting, and inspiring."
—Donyelle C. McCray, assistant professor of homiletics, Yale Divinity School, Yale University, New Haven, CT

"In your hand is a book only Leonora Tubbs Tisdale could write. In this concise yet remarkably compendious work, hidden figures become visible, muted voices speak, homiletical foremothers tutor, and readers quickly discern that women preachers are not only not going away but have a remarkable and praiseworthy preaching legacy to boast. History, or rather herstory, is recast as narrated wisdom for our times, as Tisdale weaves autobiography and curated testimony from her candid conversations with a racially, ethnically, and denominationally diverse group of women whose individual stories and unheralded service to the church and academy hand to coming generations keys for opening previously padlocked pulpits deemed off limits to preaching women."
—Kenyatta R. Gilbert, professor of homiletics, Howard University, Washington, DC; author, *Exodus Preaching* (Abingdon Press)

"*How Women Transform Preaching* is an epic homiletical 'herstory.' With wisdom and grace, Leonora Tubbs Tisdale narrates the courage and perseverance of women preachers of the past, while inspiring and uplifting women preachers in the present. This is one of those books that will be a must-read for any student of homiletics, all preachers committed to knowing the great cloud of homiletical witnesses on whose shoulders we stand, and those curious persons of faith who wonder what witnessing to the gospel requires."

—Karoline M. Lewis, Marbury E. Anderson Chair in Biblical Preaching, Luther Seminary, St. Paul, MN; program director, Festival of Homiletics; author, *SHE: Five Keys to Unlock the Power of Women in Ministry* and *Embody: Five Keys to Leading with Integrity* (Abingdon Press)

"One of the preeminent voices in homiletics shares one of its preeminent concerns: Tisdale reclaims the herstory, influence, and vitality of women preachers and teachers of homiletics who continue to shape the way we understand God and one another. Read what you've missed, be encouraged by their stories, and draw wisdom from the life-giving changes women have made in the church and world."

—Dawn Ottoni-Wilhelm, Brightbill Professor of Preaching and Worship, Bethany Theological Seminary, Richmond, IN; editor, *Homiletic* (The Journal of the Academy of Homiletics)

"Leonora Tubbs Tisdale offers an accessible glimpse into what remains an under-documented and incomplete herstory of preaching in the US. She is beckoning us toward the diversities of preaching for the ongoing transformation of preaching."

—Lisa L. Thompson, Associate Professor and the Cornelius Vanderbilt Chancellor Faculty Fellow of Black Homiletics and Liturgics, Vanderbilt Divinity School, Vanderbilt University, Nashville, TN

"*How Women Transform Preaching* is a book that had to be written, and no one is better positioned to write it than Leonora Tubbs Tisdale, one of the most gifted homiletical scholars and teachers of our generation. She brings her skills as cultural exegete, biographer, and ethnographic interviewer together in this work that analyzes and celebrates the contributions of women preachers and homiletical scholars past and present. All preachers will recognize how their own preaching is indebted, in ways they may not have realized, to canny, courageous women preachers past and present who have forever transformed the future of preaching."

—Alyce McKenzie, Le Van Professor of Preaching and Worship; Altshuler Distinguished Teaching Professor; director, Center for Preaching Excellence; Perkins School of Theology, Southern Methodist University, Dallas, TX

"Leonora Tubbs Tisdale has produced a picture of women's preaching that sings, rings true, and jumps off the page. If the title alone doesn't make your heart rise within you, then flip a few pages. Here you will find exquisite word pictures of what it looks like when women preach, thoughtful analysis of what difference it makes, and story after story of the heartbreaks and victories that accompany the task. Anyone who loves words or women or pulpits or indeed the church itself will love Tisdale's joyous telling of this important story."

—Jana Childers, dean, professor of homiletics and speech communication, San Francisco Theological Seminary, University of Redlands, San Anselmo, CA

*This book is dedicated,
with deep and abiding gratitude,
to the many women preachers, scholars, and theological students
who have courageously and boldly
lived into their callings to preach and to teach preaching,
and by so doing
have transformed our lives,
our understandings of preaching,
and our visions of God and the world*

# Contents

| | |
|---|---|
| *xi* | Introduction |
| *1* | 1. Women Preachers in the USA: A Sixty-Year Retrospective |
| *23* | 2. Reclaiming Herstory: Early Women Preachers in the USA |
| *49* | 3. US Preaching Women and the Transformation of Homiletics |
| *79* | Appendix A. Homiletical Foremothers Interviewed for This Book |
| *85* | Appendix B. Homiletical Foremothers Interview Questions |
| *87* | Appendix C. Key Dates in the History of Women's Preaching and Ordination in the USA |

# Introduction

This book arose out of my giving the Lyman Beecher Lectures at Yale Divinity School in the fall of 2019. The invitation came as I was beginning my phased retirement from Yale, where I had taught preaching for the previous twelve years. My husband and I had just moved to North Carolina to be closer to extended family, when I received a letter from Dean Gregory Sterling telling me that the faculty of the Divinity School had invited me to return to campus and give the lectures the following year.

To say that I was honored to receive this invitation would be an understatement. The Lyman Beecher Lectures are not only the longest-running lecture series in preaching in the USA (dating back to 1871) but also the most widely respected. Reading them and listening to them has long been a part of my life as a scholar of preaching, and to stand in the tradition of the outstanding scholars who had given them before me was one of the highest honors I have received as a teacher of preaching. The very first preaching book I recall reading in my seminary Introduction to Preaching class was Frederick Buechner's *The Gospel as Comedy, Tragedy and Fairy Tale*, his own Lyman Beecher Lectures from 1976. During my PhD studies in preaching at Princeton Theological Seminary, we doctoral students read a number of books written by former Beecher lecturers, including works by Phillips Brooks, P. T. Forsyth, Harry Emerson Fosdick, Paul Scherer, Gene Bartlett, Henry Mitchell, Gardner Taylor, Fred Craddock, Phyllis Trible, James Forbes, and William Sloane Coffin. While I served on the Yale faculty, I attended the Beecher lectures every year, and most years I introduced the lecturer for one of the three lectures. Included among the lecturers I heard in person were: Thomas G. Long, Renita Weems, Mary Catherine Hilkert, Eugene Lowry, Robin Meyers, Brian Blount, Anna Carter Florence, Otis Moss III, Alyce McKenzie, Peter Hawkins, and Charles Campbell. And in the intervening years (between receiving my PhD and teaching at Yale), these were some of the lecturers who graced the Marquand Chapel pulpit at Yale: Walter Brueggemann, Samuel Proctor, Ellen Davis, David Buttrick, Barbara Brown Taylor, Peter Gomes, Richard Lischer, Walter Burghardt, Barbara Lundblad, and David Bartlett. What a cloud of proclamatory witnesses!

When I first received the invitation to give the lectures, I found myself reflecting on two questions:

1. What is a topic I would enjoy researching and addressing that has not already been thoroughly addressed by the many Beecher lecturers before me? and
2. What has changed the most about preaching in my lifetime that might be an interesting and worthy topic for these lectures?

I didn't have to think long at all to realize that both the topic I wanted to address and the thing that has changed about preaching in my lifetime are one and the same. And they both have to do with *the rapidly growing numbers of women in the pulpit and in the field of homiletical scholarship in the USA and the difference those women have made in how we think about and experience preaching today.*

So when I later learned that in 2019 Yale University would also be embarking upon a university-wide celebration of women—the first women having matriculated to Yale college fifty years prior, and the first woman having entered a professional school (the school of art) 150 years prior—as a lifelong Presbyterian, I knew that these particular Beecher lectures on women and preaching must have been fore-ordained!

On a more personal note, 2019 marked the fortieth year of my own graduation from seminary and ordination to ministry in the Presbyterian

*Introduction*

# Overview of the Book

When I began reflecting on the trajectory of the three Beecher lectures, I knew that I wanted to include the following elements: some sense of the realities regarding clergywomen in the USA today—namely, how many there are proportional to men, how they are faring in their vocations relative to their male colleagues, their challenges and their triumphs; some sense of the history of US clergywomen in centuries past, especially of those trailblazers who doggedly pursued a preaching vocation in their denominations before the ordination of women was even a possibility; and some sense of the impact these clergywomen and women scholars of preaching have had on the field of preaching in general and upon the experience of those who listen to preaching today. I limited my research to US clergywomen since (a) that is the cohort I know the best, and (b) it would take a global team of scholars to do justice to a global study of women and preaching (hopefully a project for other scholars to undertake in the future).

My three lectures—which correspond to the three chapters of this book—basically developed around the foci I named at the outset. In chapter 1, I embark upon a sixty-year retrospective of what has happened to women and preaching in the US context. I begin by sharing some statistics regarding the rapid growth of women in the pulpit in the last sixty years—noting also where that growth has not taken place. Then I put flesh on those statistics by sharing the stories of some of the women who are the "foremothers" of my own professional society, the Academy of Homiletics, and have lived through those changes.

One of the major pieces of research I undertook for these lectures was to conduct interviews with sixteen of the foremothers of my professional society.[3] These interviews will eventually become a part of the permanent archives of the Academy of Homiletics, housed at the Vanderbilt University

---

3. For a complete listing of the sixteen "foremothers" of homiletics I interviewed, along with their brief bios and a list of the interview questions I asked each one, see appendixes A and B. I am deeply grateful to my colleague with whom I taught preaching at Yale for nine years, Thomas H. Troeger, for first suggesting that I might consider interviewing these foremothers. Tom has long been my best creative-ideas person, as well as a fabulous colleague and tremendous supporter of women in ministry.

## Introduction

library. I have to say that interviewing these women in my field was one of the most inspiring and moving things I have done in a long time. It was critically important to this project to have voices other than my own telling, in their own words, the stories of their varied experiences as women in ministry. And while I know this is a limited sample, it is still an important one. I suspect that many women trailblazers in preaching will find some of their life experiences—and especially the challenges they have confronted in ministry—reflected in the stories these women tell.

In chapter 2, I reflect on one of the major contributions of women scholars in the field of preaching: namely, the recovery of the histories, or "herstories," of preaching women of previous generations whose names were largely unknown to us until recent decades. When I attended seminary in the late 1970s, it was easy to believe that women had only begun preaching in the previous twenty years since women preachers of earlier eras were never mentioned in our studies. But thanks to the work of a number of women scholars in preaching and in church history, we now know better. Women have been blazing trails in the preaching of the Word for centuries. And often they have paid a very high price for doing so. In this chapter I reflect on the calls those early women received to preach and on some of the creative ways in which they found to exercise them despite the church and societal strictures placed upon them.

Finally, in chapter 3, I look at how the presence of contemporary preaching women and women scholars in homiletics—their sermons, their books, their teaching, their witness in the pulpits of the USA—has literally transformed our current understandings of preaching. I identify ten different ways in which preaching women have challenged the status quo through their preaching and have changed how we listen to sermons today. I also identify some challenges we face regarding women and preaching as we move into the future.

My hope through these lectures and through this book is to honor the many amazing preaching women who have come before us and to celebrate the gifts their dedication, perseverance, and hard work have bestowed upon us all. But as I do so, I also want to acknowledge the deep pain and anguish that some of these women, along with other marginal-

## Introduction

Church (USA). I grew up in what my husband has called "the tribe of Levites" in the Presbyterian Church with a father who was a minister, an uncle who was a minister, a maternal grandfather who was a minister, and assorted other missionaries and religious educator types in the family as well. I grew up in the bosom of the Presbyterian Church—attending Sunday morning worship, Sunday evening worship, and Wednesday night prayer meeting. My family even did "church" for vacation—going each summer to a national Presbyterian conference center in Montreat, North Carolina, where I heard a host of wonderful preachers over the years, including some outstanding African American male preachers.

But I never actually heard a woman preach—and heard it called preaching—until I entered seminary in 1975 at age twenty-four. While I was not among the first wave of women in my denomination to attend seminary at Union Theological Seminary in Virginia (now Union Presbyterian Seminary), I did ride an early wave. I recall how back in the beginning years of my ordained ministry, the women's department of my denomination published a little book of what we jokingly referred to as "baseball cards" with the names and pictures of every ordained female minister in the denomination on them. There weren't that many of us—less than one hundred in the entire southern branch of the Presbyterian Church, I'd say. The idea was that we could read through those cards and come to know one another by name.

About a decade after my ordination, when I was completing my PhD in preaching at Princeton Theological Seminary and first began attending the Academy of Homiletics (the North American professional society for teachers and scholars in the field of preaching), the women scholars who were in attendance—all six to eight of us—could easily sit around one table for breakfast. The year was 1988, and we were very much the minority in a field that had long been dominated by men.

Because of my own life experience and the challenges I have faced while becoming a preaching woman, I have long had a passion for encouraging other women in their own preaching ministries. When I embarked on my first full-time teaching job at Union Theological Seminary in Virginia, church historian Rebecca Weaver and I taught the first course ever

## Introduction

offered at that school with the word *feminist* in the title. We joked that the walls would probably fall down around us! Later we, along with another woman colleague at the newly formed Baptist Theological Seminary at Richmond across the street from us, Linda McKinnish Bridges (who several decades later became the first woman president of that institution), sponsored a conference for women seminarians and invited Yale feminist theologian Letty Russell to be our keynote speaker. I remember writing to invite her to come and basically saying, "Please. Will you come over to Macedonia and help us? We desperately need you!" God bless her! She came.[1]

In the early 1990s I joined the faculty of Princeton Theological Seminary, and it was there that I began offering a course specifically designed to encourage women in their preaching ministries. I called it Women's Ways of Preaching, and I continued to teach a version of that course through the next twenty-five years—both at Princeton and then later at Yale Divinity School. One of my major goals for that course was to encourage women in their preaching ministries and to provide a supportive environment in which they could explore issues related to the challenges they uniquely would face in ministry. Present during the week when I gave the Beecher lectures were five women who were in that very first Women's Ways of Preaching class that I taught at Princeton back in 1995:[2] women who bonded there, who all had careers as parish ministers, and who have met together every single year since their graduation from Princeton for their own week of mutual support and continuing education. They came from states all along the east coast to be present that week, and their presence—along with that of many former students, faculty colleagues, parishioners, and family members—meant the world to me.

---

1. Some years later, Katie Geneva Cannon, a pioneering womanist theologian and the first African American woman ordained in the Presbyterian Church (USA), joined the faculty of Union Presbyterian Seminary (formerly Union Theological Seminary in Virginia). The seminary now has a Center for Womanist Leadership named in her honor.

2. The women from that first Women's Ways of Preaching class at Princeton Theological Seminary who were present for the lectures were: Donna Giver-Johnston (who herself is now a scholar and teacher of preaching), Mary McKey, Diane Walton Hendricks, Tiffany Nicely Holleck, and Nancy Joyner Reinert.

ized people in the church—such as those in the LGBTQ+ community—have suffered when their own God-given callings have been denied, suppressed, or silenced. That, too, is an important part of this story.

Finally, I want to express my gratitude to the many women students I have taught through the years who have shared with me their own hopes and dreams, joys and struggles, and the many women colleagues in the field of homiletics who shared with me their own stories as I prepared these lectures. Your witness has inspired me, your faith and hope have strengthened my own, and your presence in the pulpits and classrooms of this land give visible witness to the reality that a new day for preaching has indeed dawned! Bless you, and thank you!

Leonora (Nora) Tubbs Tisdale
Clement-Muehl Professor *Emerita* of Divinity
Yale Divinity School
Currently Residing in Durham, NC
Pentecost Season, 2020

Chapter One

# Women Preachers in the USA: A Sixty-Year Retrospective

## What the Statistics Tell Us

Barbara Brown Zikmund, Adair Lummis, and Patricia Chang, *Clergy Women: An Uphill Calling*

Thirty years ago Barbara Brown Zikmund (then President of Hartford Seminary), her colleague in sociology Adair Lummis, and research associate Patricia Chang undertook what was at the time the most extensive survey of clergywomen from predominantly white Protestant denominations ever undertaken. Their research, published in the book *Clergy Women: An Uphill Calling*, summarized the findings from nearly five thousand surveys provided by ordained women and men in fifteen Protestant denominations, including the major "mainline" traditions as well as Southern Baptist, Unitarian-Universalist, and Assemblies of God denominations. These researchers did not include historically black Protestant denominations in their study since they were at the time being surveyed in another study undertaken by Delores Carpenter of Howard University—about which I will say more shortly.

The aims of the research by this team were several-fold:

- to compare statistically the numbers of clergywomen in the mid-1990s with the numbers evidenced in another study undertaken in 1977,
- to explore the ways in which various denominational procedures and practices influenced the experience of clergywomen within them, and
- to assess how successfully denominations and congregations were handling the rising numbers of clergywomen.[1]

At the time of their survey, Zikmund and her team found that United Methodists reported the largest number of ordained women overall (around three thousand[2]), followed by the United Church of Christ (around eighteen hundred) and the Assemblies of God (around sixteen hundred). However, when they looked at the percentages of clergywomen within various denominations they found that the Unitarian-Universalists had the highest percentage of women (30 percent), the UCC the second highest (25 percent), followed by the Disciples of Christ, which had 18 percent. The Southern Baptist Convention, which had formally adopted resolutions against the ordination of women, and the Free Methodist Church had the smallest percentages (fewer than 1 percent). Their study did not include Roman Catholic or Orthodox denominations who were not ordaining women at all.

Their study also showed that clergywomen were significantly underpaid relative to men (earning 9 percent less than their male counterparts in similar jobs), and that women had more difficulty finding jobs than their male counterparts—in part because denominational leadership deployment procedures consistently placed women at a disadvantage. "Clergy

---

1. Barbara Brown Zikmund, Adair T. Loomis, and Patricia Mei Yin Chang, *Clergy Women: An Uphill Calling* (Louisville: Westminster John Knox, 1998). Much of the research cited in this section is summarized in *"Clergy Women: An Uphill Calling*, an abstract of the study" written by the authors and found online at the Hartford Institute for Religion Research website, http://hirr.hartsem.edu/bookshelf/clergywomen_abstract.html, 2.

2. I have rounded off the statistics to the nearest hundred.

women," they wrote, "are unwittingly 'tracked' onto positions with less occupational status and promise."³ They also found that women were far more likely than men to become part-time pastors, to opt for employment in specialized ministries such as chaplaincy or nonprofit work, or to leave parish ministry altogether.

These researchers subtitled their book about clergywomen "an uphill calling" because they predicted that women would continue to battle practices and prejudices on the part of their denominations and congregations that would make the way forward a difficult one for them.

## Delores C. Carpenter, *A Time for Honor: A Portrait of African American Clergywomen*

In 1999, Delores Carpenter, Associate Professor of Religious Education at Howard University, published her study of clergywomen from historically Black Protestant denominations. Her findings were recorded in her book *A Time for Honor: A Portrait of African American Clergywomen*. If Zikmund's study showed that white women faced an uphill climb, Carpenter's study showed that African American clergywomen were trying to scale mountain faces.

The pay gap between clergywomen and clergymen was 15 percent in the higher ranges,⁴ clergywomen's acceptance in historically Black denominations was problematic (often with female congregants and male senior pastors being the most non-accepting), and their opportunities for serving as pastors of churches or for pastoral advancement were slim (given that congregations preferred younger male clergy as their senior pastors). Only one-fifth (21 percent) of the ordained clergywomen actually found employment as full-time pastors versus one-half (49 percent) of the male clergy.⁵ Given the reality that over half of the clergywomen were single—two-thirds of them being single mothers with children—the challenges they faced providing for themselves and their families were enormous. The

---

3. Zikmund et al, *"Clergy Women: An Uphill Calling,* an abstract," 2–3.

4. Delores C. Carpenter, *A Time for Honor: A Portrait of African American Clergywomen* (St. Louis: Chalice, 2001), 151–52.

5. Carpenter, *A Time for Honor*, 150.

majority said they acquired their primary salaries from secular jobs and worked either for free or for little pay in the church.[6]

These clergywomen also entered seminary later in life than their male counterparts (median age at admission being forty). Forty-five percent said they had switched denominations at some point, with over half of those (24 percent) saying that the desire for ordination was a major issue in doing so.[7]

These statistics give testimony to the ways in which women's experiences of call are complicated by gender formation and delayed awareness of their own gifts and abilities. When women grow up in an environment that discourages them from recognizing their God-given gifts and callings, or that openly forbids them from taking up the mantle of preacher, it takes tremendous courage, perseverance, and time for them to pursue that calling. When you add to the emotional and psychological pressures women endure—the grim realities of trying to provide for their families when jobs are scarce, salaries are poor, and positive support from parishioners is lacking—it is a wonder these women pursued their callings at all.

## Eileen Campbell-Reed, "State of the Clergywomen in the U.S.: A Statistical Update October 2018"

The latest study of clergywomen was undertaken in 2018 by Eileen Campbell-Reed, a Baptist clergywoman who describes herself as an "academic entrepreneur." When she realized that no major studies had been made of clergywomen in the past two decades, she and her research assistant sought to correct that oversight by conducting their own study in conversation with a number of denominational staff and the statistics they provided her.[8] She has published some of her most significant findings in an online article, while she works on a full-length book.

Here are some of the major findings:

6. Carpenter, *A Time for Honor*, 151–54.

7. Carpenter, *A Time for Honor*, 139–40.

8. Eileen Campbell-Reed, "State of the Clergywomen in the U.S.: A Statistical Update October 2018." The report is posted on Campbell-Reed's blogsite at eileencampbellreed.org. She reports that a book project on clergywomen in the US is currently underway.

- In 1960, the US census reported women represented 2.3 percent of all US clergy. In 2016 census reports, women represented 20.7 percent of all professional clergy.[9]
- In a number of the "mainline" denominations, the percentage of clergywomen has doubled or tripled since 1994. For example, numbers have tripled in the Episcopal Church, Evangelical Lutheran Church, and Assemblies of God.[10] Numbers of clergywomen in the United Methodist, Disciples of Christ, and Church of the Brethren have doubled, while Presbyterians (USA) grew from 19 percent to 29 percent.[11] American Baptist numbers have remained relatively unchanged the past twenty years with only 13 percent of the clergy being women.[12] On the other end of the spectrum, Unitarian Universalist and United Church of Christ clergywomen *have actually reached numerical equity with clergymen.*[13]
- In addition, their research showed that numbers were also growing in other Protestant, Pentecostal, and Peace churches. Women currently represent 30 percent of Mennonite clergy, 25 percent of Church of God clergy, and 37 percent of Foursquare clergy.[14] The statistics for Southern Baptist women are harder to track since that denomination still denies ordination to women. However, the progressive Alliance of Baptists that broke off from the Southern Baptist Convention in 1987 has women pastoring 40 percent of its congregations (it is a small denomination with only 143 congregations), and women are pastoring 7 percent of congregations in the more moderate Cooperative Baptist Fellowship. Notably, however, this study

---

9. Campbell-Reed, "State of the Clergywomen in the U.S.," 2.
10. Campbell-Reed, "State of the Clergywomen in the U.S.," 6.
11. Campbell-Reed, "State of the Clergywomen in the U.S.," 7.
12. Campbell-Reed, "State of the Clergywomen in the U.S."
13. Campbell-Reed, "State of the Clergywomen in the U.S." Italics added for emphasis.
14. Campbell-Reed, "State of the Clergywomen in the U.S."

claims that *"none of the 47,000 Southern Baptist congregations in the U.S. reportedly have female pastors."*[15]

- While the Roman Catholic Church still denies women's ordination to the offices of priest and deacon, this study notes that since 2015, lay ministers outnumber priests as designated leaders in parish ministry in the US, and 80 percent of those lay ecclesial ministers are women.[16]

Campbell-Reed also notes that "in historically Black denominations, women continue to push up a very steep hill to follow God's call into professional ministry. For example, in Black Baptist churches women represent 50-75% of church members, but less than 10% of church leadership, and perhaps 1% of pastors."[17] The African Methodist Episcopal Church offers more hopeful statistics in that a 2017 annual report on women in ministry identified thirty-two hundred women being ordained for pastoral office, and around twelve hundred serving appointments as congregational pastors.[18] Since 2000, the AME Church has also elected four women to the office of Bishop.[19]

Campbell-Reed also observed that during the past twenty years one of the biggest changes in church leadership has been the increasing acceptance of LGBTQ+ folk as ordained ministers and even, in some cases, as bishops. However, she also says that in many places, "they continue to struggle uphill in their vocations to serve churches that remain ambivalent or outright hostile to them."[20]

---

15. Campbell-Reed, "State of the Clergywomen in the U.S.," 7–8. Italics added for emphasis.

16. Campbell-Reed, "State of the Clergywomen in the U.S.," 7. These statistics come from CARA, Center for Applied Research in the Apostolate.

17. Campbell-Reed, "State of the Clergywomen in the U.S.," 8.

18. Campbell-Reed, "State of the Clergywomen in the U.S." While Campbell-Reed does not indicate what percentage of the whole these female pastors constitute, she does cite a 2016 report that estimates that women constituted more than one-fourth of congregational pastors (26 percent) in AME churches.

19. Campbell-Reed, "State of the Clergywomen in the U.S.," 8.

20. Campbell-Reed, "State of the Clergywomen in the U.S.," 9.

## Benjamin R. Knoll and Cammie Jo Bolin, *She Preached the Word: Women's Ordination in Modern America*

Finally, a book on women's ordination in America, published in 2018 by two political scientists, Benjamin Knoll and Cammie Jo Bolin, cites several additional statistics worthy of our consideration:

- A 2015 National Congregations Survey showed that while three out of five congregations in the US (around 60 percent) allow women to serve as the head clergyperson, only 11 percent of the congregations actually have women serving as the "senior or solo" pastoral leader.[21] There is a huge gap, then, between what denominations allow and what congregations actually do.

- While Zikmund and Williams found in 1990 that clergywomen made between 9 percent and 15 percent less than clergymen in comparable jobs, a 2016 study found that clergywomen made, on average, only seventy-six cents for every dollar that male clergy made (25 percent less).[22] Evidently the pay gap between male and female clergy colleagues is increasing, not decreasing.

When taken together these statistics tell a mixed tale. In some denominations, the numbers of women clergy are rapidly expanding and even reaching numerical parity with clergymen, while in other traditions they are not growing much at all and seem to have stalled.[23] Furthermore,

---

21. See Mark Chaves and Alison Eagle, "National Congregations Study" (2015), http://www.soc.duke.edu/natcong/Docs/NCSIII_report_final.pdf (May 3, 2016), as quoted in Benjamin R. Knoll and Cammie Jo Bolin, *She Preached the Word: Women's Ordination in Modern America* (New York: Oxford University Press, 2018), 10.

22. Tobin Grant, "Gender Pay Gap Among Clergy Worse Than National Average—a First Look at the New National Data," Religion News Service. https://religionnews.com/2016/01/12/gender-pay-gap-among-clergy-worse-than-national-average-a-first-look-at-the-new-national-data/ (May 3, 2016), as cited in Knoll and Bolin, *She Preached the Word*, 29.

23. A study by Knoll and Bolin, based on census data, claims that overall the percentage of clergywomen in the US has stalled at around 15 percent since the mid-1990s. See *She Preached the Word*, pp. 9–10. This finding, however, is at odds with the findings of Eileen Campbell-Reed regarding the rapid growth of women clergy in some denominations and her claim that women clergy now comprise 20 percent of the US clergy population.

Chapter One

while the numbers overall are growing, it is still the case that women are the senior or solo pastoral leader in only 11 percent of US congregations. And in the two largest church bodies in the US—the Southern Baptist Convention and the Roman Catholic church—it is still not possible for women to be ordained to ministry at all. Clergywomen are still being underpaid compared to their male counterparts. They still have difficulty getting calls as senior pastors in larger parishes, and they tend to spend longer periods of time in rural parishes or as assistant pastors than they do as solo pastors or senior pastors.

These realities are what the statistics reveal to us. But what do the women themselves tell us about becoming a preaching woman in the US during the past sixty years?

# The Stories of the Homiletical Foremothers

As indicated in the introduction to this volume, as a part of my research for this book I interviewed sixteen women who not only have been preachers themselves but also, for the most part, have pursued careers in homiletical scholarship and teaching. I wanted to hear from them—in their own voices—how this preaching journey has unfolded for them, where they have faced challenges and triumphs in ministry, and how they perceive the preaching scene for women today. My own interview sample was admittedly narrow—comprised primarily of women who have been trailblazers in the field of homiletics in the US[24]—so I certainly do not claim that these women speak for clergywomen as a whole. But their responses to the questions I asked all of them do help flesh out and amplify some of the statistics I have cited here—as well as chronicling the often-difficult life experiences that have gone on behind the scenes as these women responded to their own calls to preach. I can well imagine

---

24. For a complete listing of the homiletical foremothers I interviewed and the questions I asked them, see appendixes A and B.

that many seminarians and clergywomen will find places of identification within their stories.

## Hearing a Woman Preach for the First Time

The very first questions I asked all of the women I interviewed were: *When was the first time you heard a woman preach? And what was the effect of that experience on you?* For nearly all the white Protestant clergywomen I interviewed, the answer to the first question was very much akin to my own experience (see the introduction). These women did not hear a woman preach from a pulpit until they were young adults, often after they had entered seminary. Sometimes they couldn't even remember the first woman preacher they heard; they just knew that they had been in churches pastored by men their entire lives until adulthood.

In terms of the effect this experience had on them, Carol Norén, who is ordained in The United Methodist Church and who taught for many years at North Park Theological Seminary in Illinois, recounts that she was twenty-four years old and engaging in a seminary internship in Manchester, England, when she heard Sister Mabel Sykes, a Methodist deaconess, lead the Sunday evening service at one of the two churches she was serving. Norén says, "As she preached, I had the sensation of someone holding up a mirror, that is, 'Oh! *This* is how it looks and sounds when a woman is preaching. I wonder if that's the way I look and sound.'" She adds, "I hadn't given . . . much thought to gender and preaching before that."[25]

Lucy Lind Hogan, a recently retired professor of preaching and worship at Wesley Theological Seminary in Washington, DC, and an ordained Episcopal priest, recalls that when she entered seminary in 1976 at the Church Divinity School of the Pacific in Berkeley, California, women were not allowed to be ordained priests. They were allowed to be ordained deacons, but thus far none had been. "In fact," she says, "I thought 'Why am I doing this? I don't even know why I'm doing this.'" The first women she heard preach were her two classmates in her introduction to preaching class. There were actually four students in the class, Lucy recounts—three

---

25. Carol Norén (Wesley Nelson Professor of Homiletics, *emerita*, North Park Theological Seminary), interview questions answered in writing by Norén, November 5, 2018.

## Chapter One

women and one man and the professor who was a church musician. "We just wrote a sermon every week and preached it to each other. So basically two other women and I taught ourselves to preach."[26]

Mary Donovan Turner, who has taught preaching for nearly three decades at Pacific School of Religion, says she has no memories of the first time she heard a woman preach and surmises that it must have been while she was in seminary. All of her pastors growing up in a Disciples of Christ church in Louisiana were men, and she even says that when she last visited that church about ten years ago, it still had an all-male pastoral staff and an all-male group of elders and deacons, marching down the aisle two by two, to serve Communion.

But Turner has very early positive memories of church and being drawn toward its mysteries:

> Even as a five-year-old I was enthralled with the mystery of it. There was in the front of that Disciple church the baptistry . . . because we were immersed, and then there are these glass panels on each side of the baptistry. It is a phenomenally beautiful brick church, inside and out. . . . I still dream about it. So on Sunday morning the big organ would start playing and the minister would come through one of those glass panels that doesn't really look like a door. . . . And in my child's mind, there are all these passageways back there. It's mysterious and dark and close to God back there.[27]

Lutheran pastor and professor Barbara Lundblad, now retired from teaching preaching at Union Theological Seminary in New York, doesn't remember the first time she heard a woman preach either. But she does recall the first time she saw a woman preside at the Eucharist. It was in Marquand Chapel at Yale Divinity School in 1976 when Lundblad was a first-year seminary student and was thirty-two years old. Joan Forsberg, who had been ordained by the United Church of Christ in 1954, and who went on to serve as Registrar and then Dean of Students at the Divinity

---

26. Lucy Lind Hogan (Hugh Latimer Elderdice Professor of Preaching and Worship, *emerita*, Wesley Theological Seminary), Zoom interview by the author, December 12, 2018.

27. Mary Donovan Turner (Carl Patton Professor of Preaching, *emerita*, Pacific School of Religion), Zoom interview by the author, December 10, 2018.

School, mentoring many women students along the way, was the presider at the table.

"She was such an amazing presence," Lundblad recounts. "What I think I most remember is her presence and the way she reached out to this whole community of people. We were all gathered around the Communion table there, and she did the invitation: 'Come from the East and the West and the North and the South.' As she did that, she turned around, and I just felt like, this is the first time I have ever been invited to Communion in my life."[28]

Jana Childers, an ordained Presbyterian minister and professor of preaching at University of Redlands/San Francisco Theological Seminary, recalls growing up as a child in a conservative Pentecostal church and surviving church by regularly critiquing the sermons she experienced as being in a "manipulative style." Her first experience hearing a woman preach came just before she went to seminary. "She had red hair," said Childers (who has red hair herself). "I was just so struck with the light falling on that hair, and that face, and the fact that I was watching a woman preach. It's one of those mental snapshots that you carry all the rest of your life. She was lively and she was very sharp. Her points were very focused. I think I remember thinking, 'I don't think that I'm that focused, but I sure do like the whole idea of what she is doing.'"[29]

Christine Smith, author of the first book that addressed preaching from a feminist perspective, recalls that she was in college and on vacation at Nags Head, North Carolina, with her family when she heard that a woman who ran a beach ministry there was going to be preaching the following Sunday morning. Smith herself says that she had had a strong sense of call to ordained ministry since high school but had never before seen a woman do what she wanted to do. She announced to her family that she was going to hear this woman preach. What was it like for her? "I

---

28. Barbara K. Lundblad (Joe R. Engle Professor of Homiletics, *emerita*, Union Theological Seminary, New York), Zoom interview by the author, November 1, 2018.

29. Jana Childers (Dean, University of Redlands School of Theology/San Francisco Theological Seminary; Professor of Homiletics and Speech Communication), Zoom interview by the author, November 16, 2018.

Chapter One

think I was really overcome with joy," she said, "and with . . . some sorrow that I was in college and I had never seen a woman preach."[30]

For United Methodist Alyce McKenzie, who teaches preaching at Perkins School of Theology at Southern Methodist University, the first time she heard a woman preach was after she had been ordained and was attending a workshop led by the noted preacher and author Barbara Brown Taylor. "I was in awe," she said, "and I thought, 'Why aren't there more role models around? Where were they? Thank God I have had this experience.'"[31]

The Roman Catholic women I interviewed, both of whom are women religious, had a somewhat different experience than their Protestant counterparts regarding women and preaching.

Sister Joan Delaplane, who was the very first woman to join the Academy of Homiletics (the North American society of teachers of preaching) in 1977, and who celebrated seventy years as a sister in the Dominican Order (Order of Preachers) in 2019, recounts, "It's a good question (when I first heard a woman preach), and it's a hard one for me because growing up Catholic and having Catholic (biological) sisters, they really preached, I would say, in a different kind of way. Then I entered a community of all women who just ordinarily would speak, but they were really preaching, but we didn't call it that. I think I was never taken aback, or stunned, or in awe when I'd hear women preaching because that's just part of my life, but in a different kind of way. Not necessarily from the pulpit as it were."[32]

Mary Catherine Hilkert, professor of systematic theology at Notre Dame University and a former Lyman Beecher lecturer, is also a Dominican sister who recalls hearing her Dominican sisters preaching through the years. One of the most notable was Kathleen Cannon—now her colleague

---

30. Christine Marie Smith (Professor of Preaching *emerita* at United Theological Seminary of the Twin Cities), Zoom interview by the author, February 25, 2019.

31. Alyce M. McKenzie (George W. and Nell Ayers LeVan Professor of Preaching and Worship, Perkins School of Theology, Southern Methodist University), Zoom interview by the author, November 16, 2018.

32. Joan Delaplane, O.P. (Adrian Dominican Sister of the Order of Preachers and professor of preaching for twenty-five years at Aquinas Institute of Theology in St. Louis), Zoom interview by the author, November 12, 2018.

at Notre Dame—who led a week-long retreat for Hilkert's congregation in Akron, Ohio, where Hilkert was then serving as a school teacher. "It was a wonderful collaboration between herself and Paul Philbert, O.P., the Dominican friar she was preaching with, that gave me such a sense of the scriptures, and how she lives them, loves them." Hilkert also recalled hearing a prioress in her community who had spent much of her life in El Salvador and who had known Oscar Romero, preaching powerfully and joyfully out of a strong sense of social justice.[33]

Several of the women of color I interviewed also recalled women "preaching"—but not as ordained women and not from the pulpit.

Minerva Carcaño, the first Latina Bishop in The United Methodist Church, says that though she didn't hear women officially preaching until she was in preaching class in seminary, she had known three women—laywomen—who were local pastors and gave tremendous witness to their faith "around the edges." She also recalls how her grandmother Sophia and her mother, Rebecca, would preach to her at the table and unpack Scripture for her.

When she first heard her women classmates preach in seminary, she says, "I felt this great resonance with these women, I felt their spirit, I felt the possibility of preaching in my own voice. I found in our brothers in the class very much the model of traditional preaching and I thought, 'I'm not a man. That doesn't feel comfortable.' It didn't feel like that was a skin I could put on."[34]

Teresa Fry Brown, the Bandy Professor of Preaching at Candler School of Theology and the first African American woman tenured on that faculty, says that in her Black Baptist upbringing, though she didn't hear women doing what was called "preaching," there were women in her culture who were called "prayer warriors" who would lead testimony services. "They were doing the same thing as men were doing, but they were 'speakers.' So I heard speakers from the time I was aware I was in church." She says that her own Aunt Thelma, her grandmother's sister, was the

---

33. Mary Catherine Hilkert, O.P. (Professor of Theology, University of Notre Dame), Zoom interview by the author, December 5, 2018.

34. Minerva G. Carcaño (Bishop of the California-Nevada Conference of The United Methodist Church), Zoom interview by the author, December 6, 2018.

pastor of a church thirty-five miles from where she grew up but that the family never spoke of it and actually kept that fact a secret from her. She would hear Aunt Thelma speaking at churches, but she also reports that Thelma was never allowed to do so in the pulpit. She always had to do so from the floor.[35]

Martha Simmons is one of those African American clergywomen Delores Carpenter talks about who left her National Baptist denomination in the hopes of having more ministry options in the United Church of Christ. Simmons, the creator and director of the *African American Lectionary* and co-editor of the only African American preaching anthology to date, recalls that in her childhood, she never heard women preach from the pulpit but that she did hear women musicians *"sneak-a-preach."* Simmons says this was a common practice in African American church history:

> Women who couldn't use the title Reverend in certain circles, but who were very well liked in those circles, they didn't upset the apple cart; they'd *sneak-a-preach* while they were singing or praying. The most currently well-known preacher to do that is Shirley Caesar. I guess Shirley Caesar had been out there singing and sneaking preaching for thirty, forty years before she took the title Reverend. But I knew that woman was preaching. . . . And every time she sang, she would do it.[36]

Gennifer Benjamin Brooks, Styberg professor of preaching at Garrett Evangelical Seminary, grew up in Trinidad in the Caribbean. She recounts that the one place she heard women preaching—though they wouldn't have considered themselves doing so—was in the Evangelical Spiritual Baptist (Shouters) church. These women would preach on street corners but not in church sanctuaries. "It seemed to me," she said, "that what they preached was always very well connected to life. . . . I remember one woman coming down to the street where we lived and standing on the corner and preaching about the world . . . the state of the world. And she

---

35. Teresa Fry Brown (Bandy Professor of Preaching, Candler School of Theology, Emory University), Zoom interview by the author, December 7, 2018.

36. Martha Simmons (Creator and Director of the *African American Lectionary*), Zoom interview by the author, December 3, 2018.

saw babes with mothers in their arms. You heard what I said? Not mothers with babes in their arms. . . . That image has never left me."[37]

For Rabbi Margaret Moers Wenig, who teaches preaching and liturgics at Hebrew Union College-Jewish Institute of Religion in New York City, the path to preaching was somewhat different than that of her Christian homiletical colleagues. Wenig grew up in a secular Jewish household. She began to attend synagogue services and study with a rabbi only in high school. Her mother and aunt were pioneering feminists in their fields, so Wenig "just assumed women could do absolutely anything we wanted to. . . . It had not occurred to me that women couldn't be rabbis."[38] At the time she entered rabbinical school in 1978, there were only three women who had been ordained rabbis in the Reform movement (which began ordaining women in 1972) and one who had been ordained in the Reconstructionist movement.

The woman who was most influential in her preaching formation was Barbara Lundblad. The first congregation where Rabbi Wenig served, Beth Am, The People's Temple in Washington Heights in New York City, rented space from the Lutheran congregation (Our Saviors Atonement Lutheran Church) where Barbara Lundblad served as pastor. "For all those years," she recounts, "I not only heard [Barbara] preach. But for a number of those years, Barbara used to leave her Sunday sermon manuscript in the pulpit. And when I arrived for work on Monday, I'd find and read them. . . . Between the feedback that I received on a weekly basis from my congregation, which sat and discussed the sermon with the rabbi every Friday night following services, and Barbara's example, I began to learn a lot more about preaching than I had learned in rabbinical school."[39]

---

37. Gennifer Benjamin Brooks (Ernest and Bernice Styberg Associate Professor of Preaching and Director of the Styberg Preaching Institute, Garrett Evangelical Seminary), Zoom interview by the author, November 2, 2018.

38. Margaret Moers Wenig (Lecturer on Homiletics and Liturgy, Hebrew Union College-Jewish Institute of Religion), Zoom interview by the author, December 13, 2018.

39. Margaret Moers Wenig interview.

Chapter One

## Challenges Faced on Path to Ministry

In my interviews with these women I also asked them about the challenges they faced along the way in their own paths toward ordination.

Alyce McKenzie recounts that the obstacles she encountered were mostly internal, since she was very shy and didn't want to go into a field that required public speaking.[40]

Barbara Lundblad recounts a different internal struggle, pertaining to the whole matter of ordination itself. Before going to seminary Lundblad had worked for a number of years as a youth director in a parish in Minnesota and very much wanted to affirm the ministries of the laity. She felt that becoming ordained might be unfaithful to her affirmation of people in lay ministries and had to be convinced that this was an okay path for her to take. She recalls a panel at Yale Divinity School during her student days that helped clarify that calling for her.[41]

Linda Clader, who taught preaching for many years at the Church Divinity School of the Pacific, recounts that before she went to seminary, she was teaching Classics at a university and serving as the senior warden in her church and encountered opposition from some of the men on the vestry to having a woman in that position. "I had run into opposition about being a leader more than being an ordained person necessarily," she recounts.[42]

But once again there is something of a divide between what the white women and women of color recounted about the intensity of opposition in their ordination experiences.

Minerva Carcaño, for example, tells of the opposition she received both from her parents and from her pastor when she indicated that she wanted to go to seminary and become ordained. When her father expressed concerns about his daughter going to seminary to their pastor, the pastor told him, "Pablito, let her go. She will find a good man called by

---

40. Alyce M. McKenzie interview.

41. Barbara K. Lundblad interview.

42. Linda Clader (Professor of Homiletics *Emerita*, Church Divinity School of the Pacific), Zoom interview by the author, November 5, 2018.

God, marry him, become a good wife to a pastor and all this will be left behind."[43]

A year or so later when Carcaño was in seminary at Perkins School of Theology, the Board of Ordained Ministry from her conference in Texas came to meet with the four people from the conference who were studying at Perkins: three men and Carcaño. She recounts that she was the last to be interviewed and that at the end of the interview, the people on the board turned to her pastor—who was sitting at the table with them, since he was the registrar for ministry for the conference—and said, "Why didn't you tell us?" She realized in that moment that *her pastor had not even put her name on the list of seminarians up for ordination.*[44]

Carcaño tells that later when she was ordained and was appointed by the Bishop to serve a small new church start of thirty people in Lubbock, Texas—a church that had been abandoned by their previous pastor—she arrived in January after a snow storm. She says, "It was tremendously cold and I'm trying to build a relationship with those who were present. And I felt the coldness of their welcome with some exceptions. When I got up to preach, I noticed that they were passing a book, person to person to person to person. In some cases I could see their finger pointing to a particular place in the book and whatever they were being invited to read as I preached. I learned at the end of the worship service that it was a Bible, and they had opened it to that Pauline passage that stated, 'Women shall not speak in the community of faith.' *[T]his was my first appointment, this was my first sermon as a pastor of a church in my own right. And that was the reception. And it was [the same] every Sunday for the time I was there."*[45]

Martha Simmons, who was worshipping at a Black Baptist church in San Francisco at the time she proposed going to seminary, recalls that some people in her congregation "lost their minds" when she indicated she wanted to become ordained, and they kept asking her, "Why are you doing this? Are you sure you can't do something else?" "Finally," she recounts, "the pastor gave me a date to preach [my licensing, or initial

---

43. Minerva G. Carcaño interview.
44. Minerva G. Carcaño interview.
45. Minerva G. Carcaño interview.

## Chapter One

sermon], and the whole city was abuzz. They printed [an announcement] in the local newspaper . . . ; the place that held about two thousand people was packed. And [the pastor, at the last minute] cancelled it." This happened to Simmons several more times over the space of a number of months before she eventually did preach her sermon and was licensed to preach.[46]

Teresa Fry Brown recalls having six people in her AME ordination class: five men and herself. Fry Brown, whose husband divorced her when she decided to go into ministry, was a single mother. She said she expected opposition from men, but it was the older women in her home church who really made her life difficult. Some of them accused her of going into ministry so she could have sex with the men. Others acted out their opposition in more visual ways. "At that time," she recounts, "we were worshipping in the education building, getting ready to build a new sanctuary. Whenever I was called to read a scripture, or do a prayer [this group of women] would literally stand up and turn their backs, turn the chairs around and sit with their backs to me."[47]

Certainly some of the Protestant women had very positive experiences in their first parishes. Jana Childers happily served a small New Jersey Presbyterian congregation for several years while she was in seminary at Princeton. Barbara Lundblad ended up serving in her first parish in New York City (Our Savior's Atonement Lutheran Church) for over sixteen years.

But there were others who opted to go directly into PhD studies after seminary, in part because of the difficulty they had finding a job in a parish. Lucy Hogan recalls how difficult it was to find a job after she graduated from seminary. She said clergymen would just out and out lie to her that they didn't have jobs, and the next thing she knew, they had hired one of her male classmates.

She also recalls that after she was ordained a priest in 1982, the Episcopal bishops voted in a "conscience clause" that allowed bishops in a diocese who opposed women's ordination not to ordain women. Shortly

---

46. Martha Simmons interview.
47. Teresa Fry Brown interview.

thereafter Lucy's husband, who was a medical doctor in the Navy, was stationed in San Diego. Lucy, as a newly ordained priest from Minnesota, recalls visiting a local Episcopal church on a Sunday when the rector was absent because he was attending the church's General Convention. When he returned home, the rector called Lucy and said, "I understand you visited my church." She replied that she and her husband and son had visited. The rector then said, "I'd like to ask you not to do that again."[48] He didn't want an ordained woman worshipping in his congregation.

Christine Smith's story is the story, I fear, of far too many gay and lesbian folk who have answered the call of God to go into Christian ministry. As I've previously indicated, Chris grew up in the bosom of The United Methodist Church and felt a strong call to become a parish minister since her high school days. After graduating from seminary, she answered that call and went into parish ministry. But she says that she lived in constant fear of being outed and of losing either her church or her ordination or both. She pursued doctoral studies in preaching in order to chart a different career path for herself but testifies that her *true calling* was always to parish ministry. She later left The United Methodist Church for the United Church of Christ but also recounts standing in the midst of the seminary where she was teaching at the time she made her decision and weeping because she felt she had no choice but to do so.[49]

## The Challenges Continue

I share these stories with you because they give us just a glimpse into the reality of what contemporary clergywomen have had to go through to exercise their callings in Christ's church. And women are still struggling. I know outstanding clergywomen who, when they reach midlife, find it almost impossible to find a job in the parish appropriate for their gifts and capabilities because the preference for younger clergy or male clergy is so strong on the part of congregations. I know younger clergywomen who find that their denominations will ordain them but then give them

---

48. Lucy Lind Hogan interview.
49. Christine Marie Smith interview.

no help in finding parish-based jobs. And of course, there are still far too many LGBTQ+ clergy who live in constant fear of losing their jobs or their ordinations, or who are finding it impossible to be ordained at all in churches they dearly love.

Furthermore, there are still seminary students—including students I taught in recent years—who struggle to make their way in the church. I think of that Pentecostal student I taught who finally got her church body in Texas to ordain her but never could find a parish to serve within her denomination, so she ended up switching denominations and going through the entire ordination process all over again in the United Church of Christ. I think of that Roman Catholic Latina student I taught who had a fire in her bones to preach and finally announced to our class one day that she had begun preaching online, because God had called her and no one was going to stop her from exercising her gifts. And I think of a Korean American woman in my very last Women's Ways of Preaching class who also had a fire in her belly for preaching, who was quite a gifted preacher, but who seemed to face opposition to her voice and leadership at almost every turn.

As the statistics clearly show, we have come a long way during the past sixty years in ordaining more clergywomen, and in welcoming women into the pulpits of this land. I rejoice in and celebrate that reality. But we still have a way to go. As Lucy Hogan reminds us, "It is still the case that over half the church women of the world cannot be ordained."[50]

And a part of what we need to do is to become the best advocates we can be for opening the pulpit to all women. I was struck when I interviewed these sixteen women preachers and teachers of preaching, at how many pointed to clergymen who had mentored them in their early years in ministry, had opened their pulpits to them, and had encouraged them to become all they were created to be. I was also struck by how important to these women was the support and encouragement of women—both lay and clergy—who would advocate for them and refuse to quit pressing the church to fully embrace them and their God-given callings.

---

50. Lucy Lind Hogan interview.

Yes, we've come a long way. But before we are tempted to rest on our laurels we also need to take a look at history that predates the past sixty years—the stories of preaching women who embraced their calls long before their denominations even thought about ordaining women—and ask, "*What was it that empowered them and gave them courage to persevere in their callings when church and society so strongly opposed them? And what do we learn from their witness about how to keep persevering in our own day and time?*"

That history, or rather "herstory," is the focus of chapter 2.

Chapter Two

# Reclaiming Herstory: Early Women Preachers in the USA

In the previous chapter we looked at some statistics that show us that during the past sixty years, the numbers of preaching women have increased dramatically in the United States. In some denominations—such as Lutheran, Episcopal, and Assemblies of God churches—the numbers of clergywomen have tripled in the past twenty to twenty-five years alone. In others—The United Methodist Church, Disciples of Christ, and Church of the Brethren—the numbers have doubled. And in a few denominations—like the United Church of Christ and the Unitarian Universalists—there is now actual parity between ordained male and female clergy.

Certainly this is not the case across the board. The two largest church bodies in the US—the Roman Catholic Church and the Southern Baptist Convention—still do not ordain women at all. And in other bodies—like the National Baptist Convention—the growth in number of clergywomen has been relatively static over the past several decades. But it is nevertheless somewhat remarkable that during the sixty-year period between 1959 and 2019 *many church-going Protestants in the US have gone from seeing only men in their pulpits to hearing women preach on a regular basis.*

Chapter Two

What I will explore in the next two chapters is the question: *So what difference has the presence of these women made in how we understand and perceive of preaching?* What do we now know about preaching that we didn't know before women started preaching and teaching preaching in seminaries? And what effect has the presence of so many women in the pulpit and the academy had on how we experience the sermon itself?

# A Growing Scholarly Reclamation and Recognition of Early Preaching Women

This chapter will focus on one major shift that has occurred in our understanding of preaching: namely, the recovery of the witness of women preachers through the centuries and their histories, or, as I prefer to call them, their "herstories." When I first entered seminary in 1975 it was easy to believe that women had only started preaching a few decades before my arrival there. The only women preachers I ever heard about then were the trailblazers of my own denomination who had been ordained in the late 1950s or early 1960s. I knew their names. But when "great preachers" were discussed in classrooms, it was always male preachers: Martin Luther King, Jr., Harry Emerson Fosdick, William Sloane Coffin—to name just a few. Even in church history classes there was little to no mention of women preachers from prior centuries.

Christine Smith, a UCC clergywoman and one of the foremothers in the field of homiletics that I interviewed for this project, gives testimony that this was the case for her as well. When she went to the Graduate Theological Union in Berkeley in the early 1980s to pursue PhD studies in preaching and worship, she had to take a comprehensive exam based on six great preachers of the past. The list of preachers was all male. She reports that it was while she was preparing for that exam that she came to the decision that the place where she wanted to focus her own dissertation research, and hopefully make a unique contribution to our field, was on preaching from a feminist perspective. Her book, *Weaving the Sermon: Preaching from a Feminist Perspective*, published in 1989,[1] was the only such book we homiletical scholars had on our shelves for several decades.

It was not until I was in my first teaching assignment in the late 1980s that I learned that a branch of the Presbyterian Church, the Cumberland Presbyterian Church, had actually ordained a woman preacher back at the end of the nineteenth century by the name of Louisa Woosley. Louisa Woosley, who grew up in Kentucky, wrestled mightily with her call, suppressing it for years—until she finally ended up preaching on horseback from Kentucky all the way to the west coast of the United States. So successful was she in her ministry, in terms of both "winning souls for Christ" and raising money, that her presbytery ordained her in 1889—touching off a controversy that went all the way to the Cumberland Church's General Assembly.

Woosley's autobiography, *Shall Woman Preach? Or, the Question Answered*, first published in 1891, made a profound impact on me. It was absolutely revelatory to learn that there had been preaching women who had lived in centuries prior to the twentieth and, in Woosley's case, had even been ordained! Her book addresses objections to women preaching, based on problematic biblical texts, and her own reinterpretations of the texts. Indeed, it was when she read the Bible from cover to cover that Woosley became absolutely convinced that there were no biblical reasons given against women preaching! I am grateful to this day to another foremother of the Academy of Homiletics, Mary Lin Hudson of Memphis Theological Seminary, for writing her doctoral dissertation on Louisa Woosley, thus lifting up her life and witness for the edification of us all.

In 1997, it was a student in one of my Women's Ways of Preaching classes at Princeton Seminary[2] who first introduced me to Jarena Lee.

---

1. Christine Marie Smith, *Weaving the Sermon: Preaching from a Feminist Perspective* (Louisville: Westminster John Knox, 1989).

2. The former student who gave me a copy of Jarena Lee's autobiography is the Reverend Dr. Melinda Contreras-Byrd, who has spent her ministerial career teaching, counseling, and advocating for women of color.

## Chapter Two

Jarena Lee, an African American woman who was born to free parents in Cape May, New Jersey, was licensed to preach in the early nineteenth century by Bishop Richard Allen, founder of the African Methodist Episcopal Church. During the Second Great Awakening she preached widely in the mid-Atlantic and New England states—a dangerous venture for any woman traveling alone—sometimes even traveling below the Mason-Dixon line, where she risked enslavement as well. She, too, published an autobiography, the first published by an African American woman in the US, in which she recounts the story of her call and the diary of her many travels preaching the gospel.[3]

She recounts her call in this way:

> Between four and five years after my sanctification . . . an impressive silence fell upon me, and I stood as if some one was about to speak to me, yet I had no such thought in my heart.—But to my utter surprise there seemed to sound a voice which I thought I distinctly heard, and most certainly understand, which said to me, "Go preach the Gospel!" I immediately replied aloud "No one will believe me." Again I listened, and again the same voice seemed to say—"Preach the Gospel; I will put words in your mouth, and will turn your enemies to become your friends."[4]

I am grateful to that former student for introducing me to Jarena Lee several decades ago. But thankfully times have changed, and we don't have to rely any more on word of mouth or happenstance to learn about the "herstories" of preaching women. Women scholars in the field of preaching have, in recent decades, written books or doctoral dissertations highlighting the contributions of women preachers of prior centuries.

In 2004, Eunjoo Mary Kim, a trailblazing Korean American clergywoman and professor of preaching at Iliff School of Theology, published the first comprehensive history of women preaching, beginning with women preachers in the scriptures and the early church, and conclud-

---

3. See Jarena Lee, *The Religious Experiences and Journal of Mrs. Jarena Lee "A Preachin' Woman"* (Nashville: AMEC Sunday School Union/Legacy Publishing, 1991).

4. Lee, *The Religious Experiences and Journal of Mrs. Jarena Lee*, 12.

ing with Korean women preachers during the colonial and postcolonial periods.[5]

When Anna Carter Florence, professor of preaching at Columbia Theological Seminary (and a former Lyman Beecher lecturer), wrote her own feminist theology of women and preaching entitled *Preaching as Testimony*, she began by discussing three prominent women preachers in three different centuries of church history—Anne Marbury Hutchinson who preached in the Massachusetts Bay Colony in the seventeenth century; Sarah Osborn, who preached in Newport, Rhode Island, in the eighteenth century; and Jarena Lee in the nineteenth century—pointing to the importance of "testimony" in each of their preaching ministries.[6]

Another homiletical scholar, Beverly Zink-Sawyer, explored the intersections between preaching women and the women's suffrage movement in the nineteenth century in her book *From Preachers to Suffragists*.[7] Zink-Sawyer focused her research on women like Antoinette Brown Blackwell, Olympia Brown, and Anna Howard Shaw—all of whom saw their calling to the suffrage movement as an extension of their call to ministry and all of whom left a preaching ministry to become leaders in the suffragist movement.

And when Martha Simmons and Frank Thomas published their anthology of African American preaching from 1740 to the present, other early African American women preachers rose to the fore—Julia A. J. Foote, Zilpha Elaw, Maria W. Stewart, and Sojourner Truth—as well as more contemporary woman preachers like the late Katie Geneva Cannon, Prathia L. Hall, Barbara C. Harris, Vashti Murphy McKenzie, and Renita Weems.[8]

---

5. Eunjoo Mary Kim, *Women Preaching: Theology and Practice through the Ages* (Cleveland: Pilgrim, 2004).

6. See Anna Carter Florence, *Preaching as Testimony* (Louisville and London: Westminster John Knox, 2007), 1–58.

7. Beverly Zink-Sawyer, *From Preachers to Suffragists: Women's Rights and Religious Convictions in the Lives of Three Nineteenth Century American Clergywomen* (Louisville: Westminster John Knox, 2003).

8. Martha A. Simmons and Frank A. Thomas, eds., *Preaching with Sacred Fire: An Anthology of African American Sermons, 1750 to the Present* (New York and London: W. W. Norton, 2010).

*Chapter Two*

## Early Quaker Women Preachers

About the same time that women homiletical scholars were beginning to forefront women's herstories in their work, colleagues in the field of church history were doing the same. We have learned much from them about early preaching women in the United States. For instance, from Rebecca Larson we have learned that there were a large number of Quaker women who crossed the Atlantic from the British Isles to preach in the colonies in the early 1700s before the United States became a nation. In her book *Daughters of Light: Quaker Women Preaching and Prophesying in the Colonies and Abroad 1700–1775,* Larson estimates that between thirteen hundred and fifteen hundred Quaker women preached in the British Isles and in the American colonies in the first three-quarters of the eighteenth century.[9] They traveled the east coast of the US between South Carolina and Maine, with many of them preaching on both sides of the Atlantic Ocean. They ranged in age from seventeen to sixty-nine and came from every station of life.[10] Some were recognized by their communities on the British Isles to be "Public Friends" because of their giftedness in public speaking and vocal prayer and were sent out by those communities with formal letters of introduction to other Quaker meetings in Europe or North America.

One of these women, Rachel Wilson (1720–75), preached in places as diverse as Faneuil Hall in Boston, the New Haven, Connecticut, courthouse, the College of New Jersey in Princeton (which later became Princeton University), and the old Baptist Meeting House in Charles Town (Charleston), South Carolina. She was likened in eloquence to the popular evangelist George Whitefield, and among those to whom she preached were: then-governor of New Jersey, William Franklin (son of Benjamin Franklin);

---

9. Rebecca Larson, *Daughters of Light: Quaker Women Preaching and Prophesying in the Colonies and Abroad 1700–1775* (Chapel Hill and London: University of North Carolina Press, 1999), 63. Larson notes that "one source noted the deaths of 834 female ministers between 1700 and 1799 within the compass of the London Yearly Meeting alone. (Six yearly meetings existed in the American colonies.) Male preachers initially outnumbered female preachers on the London Yearly Meeting list, but as the eighteenth century progressed, the number of women ministers equaled or exceeded the number of men in later decades" (p. 63).

10. See Larson, *Daughters of Light*, 86.

Virginia Assemblyman Patrick Henry; then-governor of Virginia, Norborn Berkeley; and Rev. Ezra Stiles, a Congregationalist minister who later became president of Yale College.[11]

## Early Evangelical Women Preachers

In her 1998 book, *Strangers & Pilgrims: Female Preaching in America 1740–1845,* Catherine Brekus, professor of the history of religion in America at Harvard Divinity School, lifts up the preaching of evangelical women during the First and Second Great Awakenings in the US. She estimates that more than one hundred African American and white women preached in churches, at camp meetings, at outdoor revivals, and in gathering halls from the mid-eighteenth to mid-nineteenth centuries.

These women tended to come from newly formed denominations such as the African Methodists, Christian Connection, Freewill Baptists, and Millerites, who insisted that distinctions of race, class, and sex were less important than whether or not one had been saved. Among these women were: Harriet Livermore, who preached to the Congress of the United States in January of 1827 for an hour and a half; Abigail Roberts, a popular Christian Connection preacher in New York and New Jersey in the early nineteenth century whose crowds were so great she often held her meetings outdoors in fields and forests; Elleanor Knight, a Freewill Baptist preacher who served as an itinerant preacher throughout New England; and Phoebe Palmer, one of the founders of the Holiness movement within Methodism and also one of the most popular preachers of her time. Though these preaching women attracted large crowds and their influence on building up churches and inspiring their audiences was highly significant, "they were virtually written out of their churches' histories in the mid-nineteenth century—a silence," says Brekus, "that has been perpetuated ever since."[12]

---

11. See Larson, *Daughters of Light,* 233–37.

12. Catherine A. Brekus, *Strangers & Pilgrims: Female Preaching in America 1740–1845* (Chapel Hill and London: University of North Carolina Press, 1998), 7.

## Chapter Two

## Early African American Preaching Women

In *Daughters of Thunder,* Bettye Collier-Thomas tells the stories of late nineteenth and early twentieth century African American preaching women who became widely known in the US for their preaching ministries. Women like Elizabeth (last name unknown), Zilpha Elaw, Amanda Berry Smith, and Sojourner Truth—some slaves, some freed—were trailblazers who, according to Collier-Thomas,

> overcame ridicule and rejection, penury, fears of re-enslavement and discriminations, and unhappy marriages, among other obstacles. After experiences with conversion and sanctification, in which the Holy Spirit commissioned them to preach, they each set out to answer this call. Nothing could deter them—not laws and attitudes that opposed women's preaching, not even geographical limits. These women spread their message throughout the Northeast, the mid-Atlantic states, the South, the Midwest, and even across oceans.[13]

## Early Women Preachers in Europe

Even before women began preaching in the "New World," we have solid evidence that many women had already been preaching on the continent of Europe. Quaker women had been preaching in England since their founding in the mid-seventeenth century. Margaret Fell, an early leader in Quakerism who later married George Fox, was herself a preacher as well as an outspoken proponent of women preaching.[14] According to Duke historian Curtis Freeman, Puritan women were also preaching during this era on the European continent. Freeman notes that between 1640 and 1660 as many as three hundred "women prophetesses" who were radical Puritans were preaching and publishing their thoughts in Eng-

---

13. Bettye Collier-Thomas, *Daughters of Thunder: Black Women Preachers and Their Sermons, 1950–1979* (San Francisco: Jossey Bass, 1998), 55.

14. Fell's most famous publication is a pamphlet entitled "Women's Speaking Justified," in which she argued, on the basis of the spiritual equality of the sexes, that women had received the Inner Light just as men and thus were capable of being prophets.

land.[15] By the 1760s, Methodist women, such as Sarah Crosby and Mary Bosanquet-Fletcher, had moved from exhorting to preaching in England with John Wesley's approval. And as the character of Baby Suggs Holy in Toni Morrison's novel *Beloved* reminds us, though their histories are largely lost to us, women were spiritual leaders in enslaved communities long before emancipation arrived[16] and may well have been preaching in Africa long before they were forced into slavery.

## Three Types of Transitions That Occasioned the Rise of Women Preachers

In surveying this history, questions naturally arise around the conditions that allowed and encouraged women to preach. Are there any patterns that can be observed about the openings that women found for preaching, and what occasioned them?

In my own survey of these preaching women and their stories, I identify three significant types of transitions that seem to have occasioned the rise of women as early preachers in the United States: (1) ecclesial and theological transitions, (2) political and geographical transitions, and (3) personal transitions in the lives of the women preachers themselves. I want to briefly reflect on what it was about each of these transitions that made openings for women preaching possible.

### 1. Ecclesial and Theological Transitions

One of the things that stands out when reading the history of early women preachers is how often their opportunities to preach came in the

---

15. See Curtis W. Freeman, ed., *A Company of Women Preachers: Baptist Prophetesses in Seventeenth-Century England. A Reader* (Waco, TX: Baylor University Press, 2011), 17.

16. See Judylyn S. Ryan, "Spirituality and/as Ideology in Black Women's Literature: The Preaching of Maria W. Stewart and Baby Suggs Holy," in Beverly Mayne Kienzle and Pamela J. Walker, eds., *Women Preachers and Prophets through Two Millennia of Christianity* (Berkeley: University of California Press, 1998), 267–87.

midst of the emergence of a new sect or denomination. When the Spirit was "on the loose"—that is, not tamped down by church hierarchies and polity, or hemmed in by church dogmas, but allowed to manifest itself in new ways—women frequently found openings to respond to the Spirit's promptings in their own lives and to preach the gospel.

Quaker women, for instance, were encouraged to preach from their founding because of the theology embraced by their founder, George Fox. Among Quaker tenets was a strong belief that each person possessed the spirit of God within herself or himself and could rely on the Spirit of Truth—the presence of the risen Christ within—to lead him or her into all truth. "Since 'the light is the same in the male and female, which cometh from Christ,' Fox believed that, by the power of the Spirit women had the same capacity as men to voice the Word of God."[17]

Quakers did not rely on professional clergy to lead their meetings, nor did they observe sacraments such as baptism and the Lord's Supper. Instead they sat in silence, waiting for the Spirit to speak within members of the gathered community. "Since Quakers believed that inspired words came from the same source, the indwelling spirit of God, it was irrelevant who actually preached at the meeting."[18] Rebecca Larson notes that their contemporaries were often shocked by the gender equality evidenced when Quakers gathered for worship. Young girls could be quite vocal at such meetings while leading men remained silent.[19]

In *Strangers & Pilgrims,* Catherine Brekus makes the case that many of the evangelical women who preached in the US in the eighteenth and nineteenth centuries came not from the more well-established denominations (such as the Presbyterian and Episcopal churches), but from emerging sects and denominations, who believed that the end of the world was near and that women were needed to herald Christ's imminent return to earth, calling people to repentance and salvation. She writes:

17. Larson, *Daughters of Light*, 17.
18. Larson, *Daughters of Light*, 18.
19. Larson, *Daughters of Light*, 18.

> These sects invested female preaching with transcendent significance. Indeed, they did not allow women to preach in spite of their "femininity," but *because* of it. A female preacher was a religious outsider in a way that a male preacher could not be. She was a stranger and a pilgrim who had sacrificed everything—pride, money, family and security—for the glory of God. She was a "mother" or a "sister" who would nurture the family of God. . . . Most of all a female preacher was a living embodiment of Joel's promise that women as well as men would prophesy at the end time.[20]

Many of these emerging denominations were taking root among people from humble origins, and in a climate that valued heartfelt religious experience and direct divine inspiration more than theological education. Consequently they "created a religious culture in which even the most humble convert—the poor, the unlearned, the slave, or the female—felt qualified to preach the gospel."[21]

Early evangelical preaching women claimed their right to interpret the scriptures as they saw fit and defended their right to preach by reference to Old Testament leaders such as Deborah, Miriam, Huldah, and Esther, as well as to New Testament Pauline coworkers such as Phoebe and Priscilla and the four daughters of Philip.[22] They also deemed to be highly significant—as had the Quaker women before them—the prophet Joel's promise that the Spirit would be poured out in the latter days on men *and* women. More than the Quaker women before them, it was important to these evangelical women to make a biblical defense of their call—which they frequently did both in their sermons and in their written autobiographies.

In *Daughters of Thunder*, Betty Collier-Thomas notes that many of the African American women preachers of the late nineteenth and early twentieth centuries were influenced by and drawn toward the Wesleyan Holiness tradition in their preaching. For example, Julia Foote, the first woman to be ordained a deacon (1895) and the second woman to be ordained an elder in the AME Zion Church (1899), was heavily influenced

---

20. Brekus, *Strangers & Pilgrims*, 160.
21. Brekus, *Strangers & Pilgrims*, 141.
22. See Brekus, *Strangers & Pilgrims*, 217–19.

by the Holiness movement within Methodism and its perfectionist doctrines of sanctification. For more than fifty years she served as an itinerant evangelist, "traveling and lecturing widely at camp meetings, revivals and churches in California, the Midwest, the Northeast, and Canada."[23]

But Foote was not the only African American preaching woman influenced by Holiness beliefs. Collier-Thomas notes that with only one exception, all fourteen of the nineteenth- and twentieth-century preaching women she identifies in her book were associated at some point with Methodism—and many with its Holiness tradition.[24]

What were the essential tenets of Holiness belief? Collier-Thomas identifies six: "Its doctrine (1) centered around experience, (2) had roots in Scripture, (3) emphasized the work of the Holy Spirit, (4) created an aura of freedom that encouraged experimentalism, (5) had a reformist and even revolutionary nature, and (6) encouraged the formation of sects."[25]

Many of these tenets were especially conducive for encouraging the preaching of women. For example, the emphasis on a direct experience of the Holy Spirit led many preaching women to assert that they had been called by a power higher than the church—namely, by the power of God made manifest to them through the Holy Spirit—and thus had to answer that call to preach. Many of these women also claimed that they had been sanctified instantly (as opposed to the gradual sanctification over the course of a lifetime that John Wesley had espoused), had been made holy by the Spirit, and thus were liberated from the sins that might have otherwise constrained them from preaching. The revolutionary nature of the Holiness movement helped these women find the courage to leave their families and go on itinerant preaching missions for months at a time, often encountering dangers and hardships all along the way. It also em-

---

23. Collier-Thomas, *Daughters of Thunder*, 59.

24. Collier-Thomas, *Daughters of Thunder*, 15.

25. Collier-Thomas, *Daughters of Thunder*, 13. Collier-Thomas refers her readers to the following article for a deeper discussion of these six tenets: Nancy Hardesty, Lucile Sider Dayton, and Donald W. Dayton, "Women in the Holiness Movement: Feminism in the Evangelical Tradition," in Rosemary Radford Reuther and Eleanor T. McLaughlin, eds., *Women of Spirit: Female Leadership in the Jewish and Christian Traditions* (New York: Simon and Schuster, 1979), 241–49.

powered many of them to deny denominational law and polity that would restrict their freedom to preach and to take their places boldly in the pulpits of camp meetings, churches, and other venues where people gathered for worship. As Collier-Thomas puts it: "Empowered by their beliefs in holiness and sanctification, they overlooked their own hesitations about the matter. *They professed that they did not believe in having women preach, and agonized over how to preserve their marital relations and attend to their duties as wives and mothers, but then they all decided that they had to dedicate their lives to preaching the gospel.*"[26]

One of the troubling patterns that can be observed in this history is that the more the newer sects and denominational movements became institutionalized, the more the preaching of women was silenced and their preaching herstory eliminated from church records. While the Spirit was often "on the loose" in the early days of such movements—especially among poorer and less educated populations of women—over time patriarchy and hierarchy in church governments silenced their preaching and forced them to "stay in their place."

It is also important to note that few of these denominations or sects approved the kinds of structural changes that would allow women to be ordained and to perform churchly duties such as baptisms and the Lord's Supper. Consequently, itinerancy was often the only mode of preaching ministry open to them, with only a handful actually serving in local churches.

## 2. Political and Geo-political Transitions

A second type of transition that opened the way for women to preach can be seen in political transitions and the new geographies for preaching they occasioned. For instance, the establishing of European colonies in the "new world" occasioned opportunities for preaching across continents that otherwise would not have existed, and it provided fertile new soil on which European women might preach.

---

26. Collier-Thomas, *Daughters of Thunder*, 21. Italics added for emphasis.

## Chapter Two

This reality is certainly evidenced in the history of the Quaker preaching women of the 1700s. Experiencing both the "push" from the British Isles, where Quakers were legally penalized for being dissenters from the Church of England, and the "pull" to a new world where Quakers not only dominated the colonial governments of Pennsylvania and Rhode Island, but also served New Jersey and North Carolina governments in significant numbers,[27] Quaker women—often with the blessing and endorsement of their meeting houses in the British Isles—preached throughout the colonies in the eighteenth century. As Rebecca Larson notes, "Quakerism, with its unpaid, travelling ministry, 'requiring no church building, a minimum of organizational apparatus, and offering a faith shorn of liturgy, sacraments, and an intricate theology' was uniquely suited to colonial American circumstances."[28] These travelling Quaker women were known for their plain dress, their radical faith, and their eloquent speaking. They attracted large audiences and made strong positive impressions not only on women but also on leading men who came to hear them as well.

Another example of how geo-political realities opened the way for women to preach is witnessed in the westward expansion of the American frontier in the nineteenth century. Here—as in the case of the early Quaker preaching women—political and ecclesial realities were often intertwined in opening the way for women to preach. For example, because there were not enough seminary-educated men willing to preach in the western territories, some denominational bodies began waiving their high standards for clergy education—which opened the door for women's proclamation. One such example can be found in the Cumberland Presbyterian Church, a group that broke away from the Presbyterian Church USA because it advocated less stringent clergy education, greater sympathy for some of the Great Awakening revival techniques, and greater doctrinal freedom of expression. As I've already mentioned, Louisa Woosley from Kentucky traveled by horseback for many years in order to preach in the western ter-

---

27. Rebecca Larson notes that half the population of Newport, Rhode Island, was Quaker in 1704 and that Quakers also controlled half the seats in the North Carolina General Assembly in 1703. Some historians have referred to this era as "the Golden Age of Quakerism in America." See *Daughters of Light*, 3–5.

28. Larson, *Daughters of Light*, 7.

ritories in the late nineteenth and early twentieth centuries.[29] By age fifty, she had preached 6,343 sermons, witnessed 7,664 professions of faith, and baptized 358 people in thirteen states.[30]

Of course, not all geo-political realities in the US were conducive to women preaching. Catherine Brekus notes the tremendous risks African American evangelical preachers of the early nineteenth century took when they dared on occasion to preach below the Mason-Dixon line in states where slavery was the norm. Furthermore, she notes that most of the evangelical preaching women before the Civil War came from the northern US states, and not from the more conservative southern states where societal pressures were stronger on women to stay in their place.

## 3. Personal Transitions in the Lives of Early Preaching Women

What empowered these women to preach, and what gave them courage to do so in the face of tremendous ridicule, persecution, and opposition, was their deep-seated belief that they had been called by God to do so. Whether it was through a dream, a vision, or a personal encounter with God while fully awake; whether the call came through study of the scriptures or while at prayer or during a religious meeting, evangelical preaching women consistently testify in both their sermons and their autobiographies that it was God who had called them to preach and that they had had nothing whatsoever to do with that call. Indeed, many describe themselves as being poor, uneducated, and lacking in eloquence, and marvel at being called in spite of their many limitations.

---

29. In her autobiography, Louisa Woosley reports that during the first four years of her ministry she preached 912 sermons "for which God has given me two souls each." Indeed, she could not answer positively all the invitations she received to preach. Over five hundred new members were received into the Cumberland Presbyterian Church through her ministry during that four-year period. See Louisa M. Woosley, *Shall Woman Preach? Or the Question Answered* (Originally published in 1891 by Louisa Woosley. Reprinted in Memphis: Frontier, 1989), 100–101.

30. See Donna Giver-Johnston, *Call the Question: Reclaiming a Rhetorical Witness of Women's Claims to Preach in Nineteenth-Century America for Contemporary Homiletics* (PhD dissertation at Vanderbilt University, 2014), 203.

Yet despite that strong sense of call, many of these women delayed answering it for months or even years because of the opposition they faced. Writes Brekus: "Nancy Towle [a nineteenth-century nondenominational preacher] debated for two years before finally becoming an itinerant; Jarena Lee waited eight years to take up her calling; and because she was illiterate and a slave, Elizabeth [a late eighteenth-century African Methodist preacher] procrastinated for twenty-nine years."[31]

What is even more striking, however, is that in nearly all the recorded cases, evangelical women only began preaching after significant illness or tragedy struck their lives. Louisa Woosley recounts going through several serious battles with physical illness, including one in which "I was reduced to a frame, and as helpless as an infant" before finally acquiescing and agreeing to preach the gospel.[32] Ellen Stewart, a Methodist from Ohio, "tried to quench the spirit by choosing to get married rather than to preach, and as a result, she sank into a deep depression." It was not until two years later that she began preaching.[33] Elleanor Knight (a Christian Connection preacher) had suffered abuse from her husband[34] and had lost two children to death—children she believed God had taken away from her as a result of her spiritual disobedience—before she actually began preaching.[35] Jarena Lee lost her husband and several children to death and was supporting two infant children alone when she finally began itinerant preaching.[36] And Zilpha Elaw, an early nineteenth-century African Methodist preacher, almost died from an internal inflammation before commencing her preaching ministry.

One cannot help but wonder, when reading the stories of these women, how much the societal pressures to conform to the "feminine"

---

31. Brekus, *Strangers & Pilgrims*, 190. Material in brackets added.

32. Louisa M. Woosley, *Shall Woman Preach?* 98–99.

33. Brekus, *Strangers & Pilgrims*, 189.

34. Brekus, *Strangers & Pilgrims*, 177.

35. Brekus, *Strangers & Pilgrims*, 191.

36. Dennis Dickerson, "Foreward," in Jarena Lee, *Religious Experiences and Journal of Mrs. Jarena Lee, "A Preachin' Woman"* (Nashville: AMEC Sunday School Union/Legacy Publishing, 1991), x.

norms of the day, and the ecclesial roadblocks raised to their preaching as women, contributed to their illnesses of mind and body and to their despair. Pressured to marry and have children, ridiculed and admonished for "exposing themselves" when they dared speak in public, and encouraged to live into a feminine ideal of subservience, piety, and humility, these women faced obstacles at every turn. *What is remarkable is that they nevertheless persevered,* believing in their heart of hearts that they would be forsaking God's calling upon their lives if they did not, seizing the openings available to them (while pressuring for more), and trusting the Spirit to empower them and give them the words to proclaim.

## Lessons Learned from Herstory

So what might we in the church today learn from this history of early women preachers in the US?

1. *God's spirit rests on people the church doesn't expect to be called to preach, and we need to be open and attentive to the Spirit's often unorthodox movements.*

For starters, we are reminded that God's spirit not only rests upon those whom our church bodies deem to ordain through official channels, but also upon countless others who may not seem educated enough, doctrinaire enough, or the right gender, race, class, or sexual orientation to meet our fallen human standards. It was through the ministry of Spirit-anointed laypeople, women and men, that the church of Christ was first given birth, and as this history reminds us, it is often through the preaching of Spirit-anointed laypeople of all varieties that the church continues to be reborn and renewed.

In her recent book *The Censored Pulpit*, Donyelle McCray, who teaches homiletics at Yale Divinity School, makes a convincing case that the medieval visionary Julian of Norwich was not only a "mystic," as people often refer to her, but also a mystical *preacher* who, through her life lived in prophetic vocation as an anchoress, and through her visionary writings, *preached* from her anchorhold in Norwich, England.[37] In the final chapter of her book, McCray urges us to expand our usual definitions of preaching to recognize that there are many people today—including many laypeople—who, like Julian, are not preaching in pulpits in church sanctuaries or in modes and forms we usually associate with "preaching," but who nevertheless are *preaching* through their lives and their oral and written witness. One of the examples she names is that of the British retreat leader and author of retreat meditations, Evelyn Underhill, who was herself heavily influenced by Julian's witness. Another is Mother Willie Mae Ford Smith (1904–94), a twentieth-century gospel singer who embodied the "sneak-a-preach" mode of preaching of which Martha Simmons speaks, in which Smith would sing a gospel song that included within it, somewhere along the way, a brief sermonette. "Smith did not see herself as a singer alone"; writes McCray, "she considered herself a preacher and evangelist. Her experience illumines an often-overlooked form of preaching undertaken by African American Women."[38]

From our survey of women preachers in the US, I think we could add to McCray's list of those who preach outside the box, often as outsiders. Our list might include those Catholic women who have been preaching to one another in convents for centuries or who preach in local congregations today—though not ordinarily at the Eucharist. We could include those women who preach on the internet, or at coffeehouses, or in other non-church locales because their denominations won't ordain them. Our list might include those women who have preached through their own devotional writings or who, during the Bible studies they lead, often blur the lines between preaching and teaching.

Perhaps, rather than bemoaning the increasing number of "uneducated" laypeople who are serving pulpits in geographical areas underserved by ordained clergy, seminaries and seminary-trained clergy should be celebrating and encouraging them and offering ongoing training for them. Perhaps rather than jealously guarding local parish pulpits, pastors should

---

37. Donyelle C. McCray, *The Censored Pulpit: Julian of Norwich as Preacher* (Lanham, MD and London: Lexington Books/Fortress Academic, 2019). See chap. 6, "Trajectories: A Mystical Homiletic," 101–20.

38. McCray, *The Censored Pulpit*, 16–17.

be opening them, from time to time, to laypeople both within and without their congregations, who have received a Word from God that they are led to bring to the gathered community of faith. Rabbi Maggie Wenig's practice of inviting laypeople in the congregation to preach on the Yom Kippur holiday afternoon—a practice I will say more about in chapter 3—is one Christian pastors might also emulate. And perhaps rather than viewing preaching primarily as a clerical calling, we—who believe the Spirit has indeed been poured out on *all flesh*—should reclaim it as a calling of the whole people of God.

2. *When the Spirit says "preach," you gotta preach—even if that calling is delayed, opposed, or redirected.*

The second thing this survey of past preaching women would suggest is that when the spirit of God rests upon a woman—or anyone, for that matter, whom church and society deem "unworthy to preach"—and calls her to preach, not responding is not an option. Ultimately—for the sake of her own soul and her own faithfulness to God—she must respond. The only questions are: When? Where? To whom? And how?

These stories give testimony to the fact that women have sometimes had to wait years to have their calls affirmed and to find openings for preaching. In the process they have endured physical and mental illnesses, the deaths of loved ones, divorce, separation, and the ridicule of those they loved and looked to for spiritual guidance. They have survived enormous financial hardships and have had to depend upon the kindness of strangers to house and feed and care for them while undertaking their itinerant ministries. They have also had to entrust the care of their infants and children to supportive family members and friends and have gone weeks and even months at a time without seeing their loved ones. They have, in short, suffered heartbreak after heartbreak, challenge after challenge, setback after setback. Yet the call of God, and the power of the Spirit at work in their lives, nevertheless gave them strength to persevere and the courage to persist in living into their calls.

Furthermore, the openings to preach for these women have not always come at their own back doors. Preaching women, as we have seen,

## Chapter Two

have crossed oceans on slow boats, crossed mountains and rivers on horseback, and crossed a lot of dangerous, rugged terrain on foot to find those people who are eager to hear the word of God from their lips. But find them, they have—in places as diverse as open fields and forests, town halls, university campuses, congressional chambers, churches, and lecture halls. And crowds of people have come to hear these women—sometimes themselves traveling for days to arrive at a place where they could camp in the open and be fed by the spirit of God at work in the lives and words of these preaching women.

It is also important to note to whom these women have preached. Yes, they have sometimes preached to the high and mighty of society (as is the case with some of the women we discussed in this chapter), but more often they preached to the poor, to the uneducated, to recent immigrants, and to those who did not fit into the mainstream churches of their day. They preached to rebels and misfits, to pioneers and trailblazers, to farm workers and ex-prisoners and day laborers—basically to anyone who would show up and listen to them. By so doing, they have followed in the footsteps of Jesus himself, who was known to be the preacher for the common people and who sometimes had no place to lay his head. From their testimonies, and the testimony of others who marveled at their faithful witness, we know that many of the people who came to hear these women preach had their lives turned upside down, just as lives were upended by the preaching of Jesus.

Finally, it is important to note how these women preached. They had no computers or iPads or access to the latest commentaries that theological libraries had to offer. Rather, they interpreted what they did have—the word of God as revealed to them through the Scriptures and the Spirit—simply, plainly, and passionately. Their sermons were down to earth, preached in the common language of their people, without great adornment. Consequently, they remind us all of the basic tools needed for preaching: a willing preacher, a Bible, a listening congregation, and the power of the Holy Spirit, working within us, among us, and through us more than we can ask or think.

3. *Great harm is done to those women whose calls to preach are denied or opposed by the church.*

This history also reminds us of the deep harm that is done to those in our midst who are called by God's spirit to preach, but who, on the basis of gender (or race, sexual orientation, class, differing abilities) are denied the right to preach. The history of these early preaching women gives testimony that such denials have, in the past, led to serious illnesses of the body, mind, and spirit. Women have suffered—and suffered mightily—by the refusal of churches to allow them to do what they believe in their hearts God has called them to do. And, according to Bp. Minerva Carcaño, clergywomen are still suffering illness in disproportionate numbers today. Says Carcaño:

> At every place that I've been as a pastor, then as a District Superintendent and now as a bishop, a thread that weaves throughout the experience of ministry for myself with colleague women has been illness. Illness of different degrees. Some of it very serious illness like cancer. And we have gathered to talk about it as pastors, as superintendents, as bishops because we have felt that. We have felt that the burden of continuing to have to challenge systems that are still committed to keeping the voice of women out or quieted even is very damaging to . . . the spirit and even the body of women. And we need to be attentive to that and help each other.[39]

Perhaps it is time for mainline denominations, who have in recent years celebrated the anniversaries of the ordination of women, publicly to repent of their past histories of discrimination against women and suppression of women's voices in the pulpit. And perhaps it is time for denominations who still deny ordination to women and marginalized others to do some serious soul-searching about the harm they are causing not only to women but also to the church as a whole in the process. For let us not forget: when we fail to ordain half of the human race and acknowledge their callings as preachers of the gospel, it is not only the women or LGBTQ+ communities who suffer; the whole church of Christ loses voices critical to its understanding of the whole gospel of God.

---

39. Minerva G. Carcaño (Bishop of the California-Nevada Conference of The United Methodist Church), Zoom interview by the author, December 6, 2018.

## Chapter Two

Sister Joan Delaplane of the Dominican Order of Preachers, the first woman member and president of the Academy of Homiletics, told me a story during my interview with her that continues to haunt me and that speaks eloquently both to the harm done to women today who are called to preach and have that call suppressed, and to the harm done to the church when women are not allowed access to the pulpit. Sr. Joan recounts a time in her life when she, a Dominican sister, had just finished a forty-day retreat and had spent an entire day meditating on the scripture passages assigned by the lectionary for the upcoming Sunday. "It was very profound. It was wonderful," she said. "And I was so excited because there was no priest at this retreat center that day, so we were going to go down to a neighboring church. They had a 5:00 Saturday night liturgy, so we were going to that mass."

She recounts how the preacher at this church gave the announcements and then "literally just read the scriptures at us." "Then he said, 'You know, it's too hot. We're going to skip the preaching today.'" Sr. Joan comments: "Now it was about 80 degrees. It was comfortable and lovely. 'But (the preacher continued) let me tell you this joke I heard.' Then, after telling a joke that wasn't humorous, he said, 'Oh, and let me tell you about the nuns down the road. They had a swinging party for this Jubilarian. I'm telling you, you should've seen that table. Today they've got six gals entering that community, and I want you to know they're good looking gals.'"

Sr. Joan recounts,

> I was shaking. I was literally shaking in the pew. I was so upset and so angry. This is [the Lord's Day], the only time the people of God can get nourished by the Word of God. [The Word for the day] was so profound and beautiful, and this is what they had to sit through. Now this is my one and only time with [this priest]. I'm leaving. I'm getting out of there, but my pain, when you talk about pain, it's a pain of the people who are experiencing this kind of famine from not being fed by the Word. . . . I sat there, teaching preaching, gifted to be able to preach, having spent the whole day on that Word. I would have loved to have been able to share it, but the one test that I failed in the seminary was anatomy. That's sad.[40]

---

40. Joan Delaplane O.P. (Adrian Dominican Sister of the Order of Preachers and professor of preaching for twenty-five years at Aquinas Institute of Theology in St. Louis), Zoom interview conducted by the author, Part I, November 8, 2018.

The kinds of stories of women and their calls that historians and homileticians have been reclaiming for us are not just stories of the past; they are sadly stories of the present as well. And if you ask me, the church has a lot of repenting to do—not just for what it has done to women, but for what it has done and continues to do to the whole body of Christ by denying the witness of women from its pulpits.

4. *We are called to identify key moments of transition that provide openings for women preachers today.*

Finally, this history calls us to become as wise as serpents in our readings of the times and our identification of those moments of transition that can be openings for people on the margins to preach.

I think, for example, of that Roman Catholic Latina seminarian I taught some years ago who had a burning in her bones to preach but loved her church too much to leave it. She seized upon the internet as a place where she could do so freely and publicly, and developed a blog site where she could preach and enter into dialog with people the world over about her sermons.

Another former student of mine, who grew up Pentecostal but most recently pastored a small UCC Church in New York state, had a passion for reaching unchurched millennials with her preaching. They were not present in great numbers in her small congregation on Sunday mornings. So she began videotaping her sermons each week and then posting them on Facebook. As a follow-up, she has engaged in dialog with her millennial followers about the concerns raised in her sermons.

I also think of a third former student—now a chaplain at a large female undergraduate institution in Georgia—who has established a blog site to promote African American women and their preaching. She has also recently published a book of her own wonderful sermons.

All of these women are exemplars of what homiletician Martha Simmons thinks is a wave of the future for clergywomen—especially women from churches whose denominations refuse to ordain them. Of all the homiletical foremothers I interviewed, Simmons was the most pessimistic about ever seeing significant change in the Black Baptist denomination in which she was raised. She frankly told me that she thought I could come back and ask her the same questions in another twenty years and that nothing much would have changed with the Baptists or the Church of God in Christ (the largest Black denomination). Simmons herself charted her own path of writing and preaching and publishing largely outside of official church channels, and while she admits that it has had its ups and downs, she has also found the freedom to work on her own terms very fulfilling. She is strongly encouraging the younger clergywomen she mentors these days to see the internet as a space where they can freely preach the gospel entrusted to them and even build church communities for the future.[41]

These women, it seems to me, are following in the footsteps of their female preaching ancestors of earlier centuries—taking those openings that are available to them in this time of technological transition in our world—and using those openings to foster women's preaching of the gospel.

## A Final Personal Postscript

In a book he wrote about one branch of our family's history, my (now deceased) maternal grandfather, Dr. James English Cousar, Jr., recounts that two Quaker preachers from Ireland—Mary Peisley and Catherine Payton—visited a colony of Quakers living in the area now known as Camden, South Carolina, in December of 1753 and preached there for twelve days. Among the settlers was a family of Englishes, my ancestors, who had immigrated to the new world from Ireland only five months prior.

My grandfather, a conservative Presbyterian minister who opposed women's ordination (including my own) until the day of his death, comments on the courage of these women and the hardships they must have endured as they traveled the 125 miles from Charleston to Camden, covering territory that had no road going through it until that very year. (Talk about literal trailblazing!). He also surmises that several of the youth in

---

41. Martha Simmons (Creator and Director of the *African American Lectionary*), Zoom interview by the author, December 3, 2018.

the English family were probably among those converted by these women and their preaching. Yet when it comes to giving reasons for the decline of Quakerism in South Carolina later in that same century, he concludes, "Such itineration as was undertaken by Mary Peisley and Catherine Payton, *besides laboring under the prohibition expressly laid down in Scripture* (1 Timothy 2:12-14), was not suited to the pioneer life of South Carolina at that period."[42]

I cannot help but wonder, however: would I have been doing what I've done throughout my ministerial career—preaching, teaching preaching, and undertaking research in the field of homiletics—had it not been for the courageous witness of those early Quaker preaching women? I also cannot help but wonder: how many of us reading these words come from families where preaching women, at some point along the way in our family histories, brought the gospel to bear in such persuasive, inspired, and Spirit-filled ways that lives were changed, faith was kindled, and new life paths were charted?

I thank God for those early US preaching women! And I also thank God for the revolution in scholarship about women and preaching that has begun during the past several decades that has allowed their stories to come forward so that all of us can begin to get to know them and find our own courage and resolve strengthened through their witness.

---

42. James English Cousar, Jr., *Quaker Turned Presbyterian: The Spiritual Pilgrimage of Robert ("Robin") English* (self-published; copyright 1956), 12. Italics added for emphasis.

Chapter Three

# US Preaching Women and the Transformation of Homiletics

In 1983, I, a newly ordained Presbyterian minister and co-pastor with my husband, Alfred, of four small churches in central Virginia, was elected a delegate from the Presbyterian Church (USA) to the Sixth Assembly of the World Council of Churches in Vancouver, British Columbia. Frankly, attending that meeting and being immersed for ten days in worship and Bible study and conversations about the issues facing our world with Christians from all over the globe was one of the great highlights of my life.

Our worship that week took place in a huge yellow-and-white-striped circus tent set up on the campus of the University of British Columbia. On Sunday, the World Council was able to celebrate the Eucharist together for the first time because of the *Baptism, Eucharist and Ministry* document that had already been studied and discussed by the member denominations for several years. Not everyone there participated in the eucharistic part of the service; some intentionally opted out. But for the first time, Christians who wanted to participate in a global, ecumenical celebration of the Lord's Supper on a scale never before envisioned were invited to do so.

While I have forgotten a lot of what happened in that service, I have not forgotten its spirit. People literally came from north and south and east and west to partake together at the table spread before us in the name of Christ. They came dressed in the finest from their diverse cultures, as musicians from around the globe led us in lively hymns and songs. Scripture was read and prayers offered in multiple languages. And a highlight of the service was when all of us said aloud together the Lord's Prayer, each of us in our own language.

But the visual I most remember from that service was of two of the six celebrants, standing side by side at that table with the emblem of the WCC—a ship setting sail with a cross as its mast—behind them, issuing the invitation to us all to come and partake of the table Jesus had spread before us. One of the celebrants was Robert Runcie, then Archbishop of Canterbury. But the other was a woman—a Danish Lutheran clergywoman standing there in her beautiful long white clerical robe with a ruffled collar—co-presiding at Christ's table. For many people who were present that day, I suspect it was the first time they had ever been at table with a woman celebrating.

I wrote an article for one of our church's publications about that experience and titled it "A Taste of Heaven." For in many ways I glimpsed that day worship as expansive and inclusive and celebratory as any I expect to experience on this earth. And the presence of that Danish woman pastor at that Communion table—where Catholics and Protestants, Orthodox Christians and Pentecostals all gathered that day—was an important visible sign that the old era of a male-dominated clergy was coming to an end and that a new inbreaking of God's inclusive reign was coming into existence. I knew, even then, that preaching and worship would never again be the same.

## The Transformation of Preaching

In this chapter I want to talk about the transformation of preaching as it has happened in this small part of this globe—the United States of America—as a result of the ordination of clergywomen. To assist me in this task, I asked each of the sixteen foremothers of homiletics in the US that I interviewed for these lectures this question: *From your vantage point, what difference has the presence of so many clergywomen and women homiletical scholars made in how we experience and perceive preaching today?* The women I interviewed had varied answers to that question. But what I want to do is focus on ten significant changes they and I have identified, and then invite us all to think about how the presence of women clergy has literally transformed homiletics during the past sixty years.

## #1) Clergywomen as Role Models for Girls (and Boys)

The first change I note may be obvious, but that does not discount its importance. The sheer presence of women and womanly bodies in the pulpit has, for many young girls and young women, completely transformed their understanding of who can speak for God.

Gennifer Brooks, professor of preaching at Garrett Evangelical Seminary, put it this way:

> Visibility, just the visibility of women . . . does something for the Church. . . . [I]n the [Black] Baptist Church being the first lady is a big thing. But the identity of the first ladies comes out of the [male] pastor. The fact that we women can take our place in the front seat and can actually be the voice of God, the voice that represents who God is. That's what's important. And that is what makes a difference.[1]

Several women I interviewed talked about the vocational pathways that are now opened to girls by the sheer presence of women in ministry. While many of these homiletical foremothers never themselves heard a woman preach until adulthood, they rejoice that we are now raising generations of young women who have known the presence of women in the pulpit and at the altar and Communion table since childhood. And what a difference that presence makes for how young women view their own vocational options.

Martha Simmons, creator of the *African American Lectionary*, thinks it makes a difference for opening not only the pathways to ordained ministry

---

1. Gennifer Benjamin Brooks (Ernest and Bernice Styberg Associate Professor of Preaching and Director of the Styberg Preaching Institute, Garrett Evangelical Seminary), Zoom interview by the author, November 2, 2018.

## Chapter Three

but also the vocational path toward theological scholarship of all varieties. Says Simmons, "I think the increased numbers of women in the pulpits also helped to boost the number of women scholars, period. Young girls went to church, saw women, and said, 'Well, I may not want to be a preacher, but I want to teach.' . . . I'm so excited by the young scholars that have come through in the last fifteen years, and I believe that they saw women in the pulpit and said, 'I believe I can do that (I can do ministry); I can do that.'"[2]

Recent statistical studies bear out, in a more systematic way, the significant ways in which having clergywomen as mentors in early life transforms the lives of children, youth, and young women. Two political scientists, Benjamin Knoll and Cammie Jo Bolin, recently undertook studies of women and men to see how their experience with male and female clergy growing up had affected their self-esteem (that is, their own sense of self-worth). They found that for women self-esteem overall increased 18 percent when they had significant female clergy leaders in their youth over the women who had experienced only male congregational leaders. Interestingly, they found that for men self-esteem was not perceptibly changed one way or the other by whether they had male or female leaders. These authors go so far as to say in summary, "*The self-esteem gap between men and women might be eliminated entirely in a world where women have female clergy at least 'some of the time' in their formative years.*"[3]

In addition, Knoll and Bolin found other interesting evidence of the influence of clergywomen on girls' and women's lives. They found, for instance, that "women, whose most influential religious congregational leader growing up was a woman receive, on average, *one additional year of schooling over women whose most influential leader was a man*" (16.2 years of education versus 15.1 years).[4] I cannot help but note that that one year could well mark the difference between graduating from college or not.

---

2. Martha Simmons (Creator and Director of the *African American Lectionary*), Zoom interview by the author, December 3, 2018.

3. Benjamin R. Knoll and Cammie Jo Bolin, *She Preached the Word: Women's Ordination in Modern America* (New York: Oxford University Press, 2018), 130–31. Italics added by the authors.

4. Knoll and Bolin, *She Preached the Word*, 135. Italics added for emphasis.

Furthermore, while Knoll and Bolin found in their survey that 61 percent of women and 74 percent of men reported that they were currently employed full-time outside the home—a gap of 13 percent—that gap entirely disappeared when a woman reported that her most influential religious leader growing up was also a woman. "Those women," they report, "are employed at the same rate as men."[5] These findings seem to reinforce Martha Simmons's observation that having clergywomen as pastors not only opens religious vocations as an option for girls and young women, but also it opens them to receiving further education and pursuing other full-time vocational options as well.

Furthermore, while these scholars give evidence that the presence of women in the pulpit does not negatively affect boys' self-esteem, I cannot help but wonder what it does *positively* for young boys and their future openness to women's leadership and mentorship in all areas of life. We live in an era where, as the "Me Too" movement and national discourse at the highest levels have clearly shown us, misogyny is far from dead. And its evil, vitriolic effects are experienced not only by young girls but also by young, impressionable boys. I cannot help but think that seeing women as trusted religious leaders in their youth must have many positive effects on boys and young men as well and influence the ways in which they treat women in their adulthood. I am hopeful that in the future, studies might be undertaken that assess those positive effects as well.

## #2) Clergywomen and Expanding God Imagery

Certainly the presence of women in the pulpit, speaking on behalf of God, ultimately affects the way in which people perceive God as well. I remember how a young boy in one of the churches my husband served as pastor used to mistake him for Jesus with his brown hair and beard (not to mention his tender kindness). "Mommy," he said when my husband went to pay a pastoral call on the family one afternoon, "Jesus is here! Go let him in!" In like manner I remember how stunned I was the first time a mother in one of the first churches I was serving as pastor presented me

---

5. Knoll and Bolin, *She Preached the Word*, 135.

with a picture her four-year-old son had drawn of his pastor. There I was, with my long brown hair, sitting on the floor with the children during our weekly children's sermon, surrounded by all the holy trappings of church, with a light glowing over my head. At some visceral level I knew then that that little boy's vision of ministry—and of who can speak for and represent God—was slowly but surely being changed by having a woman in his pulpit at a very young age.

Sr. Joan Delaplane, retired professor of homiletics from Aquinas Institute, laments the fact that children in Roman Catholic churches often do not have the experience of seeing women speaking for God—especially during the mass. She comments: "One of the things that is painful, is that people in the pews, women in the pews and children, young people, they don't see the woman up there, and then how their image of God can also represent the one who speaks for God. There is a sadness for me that they do not experience or think of an image of this great God in any female terms."[6]

Certainly having women in the pulpit is not the only way to expand God imagery for children and adults. Expanded awareness of God's being can also take place by the intentional use of inclusive God language in worship and liturgy, by the use in sermons of varied images for God—including female images—and by Bible-teaching to children that stresses the faithful leadership of women as well as men and that lifts up female imagery for God that is present in scripture itself (such as God as a mother hen, gathering her chicks to herself).

In her book entitled *SHE: Five Keys to Unlock the Power of Women in Ministry*, Karoline Lewis, professor of preaching at Luther Seminary in St. Paul, Minnesota, summarizes what is at stake in women claiming their rightful places in ministry in this way:

> Women in ministry give witness to the breadth and depth of what we dare to imagine is the potential and possibility of God's grace. When our voices are sidelined, when our presence is questioned, when our presentation of

---

6. Joan Delaplane, O.P. (Adrian Dominican Sister of the Order of Preachers and professor of preaching for twenty-five years at Aquinas Institute of Theology in St. Louis), Zoom interview by the author, Part I, November 8, 2018.

the gospel is called into question it is never, ever just about us. *It is also about the imagination of God.* When our imagination for God's hope for the church is undermined by our lack of imagination, that is when God becomes less than God.[7]

## #3) Women's Embodiment in Preaching

Karoline Lewis also links Jesus's own incarnation with the necessity for women's embodiment in preaching. "Preaching," she writes "is a necessary act for understanding the theological promise of the incarnation. The Word becomes flesh again in proclamation, incarnated anew in the body. To take the incarnation seriously means that we have to take our bodies seriously."[8]

This is true. But it is also true that taking their female bodies into the pulpit has not always been easy for women. As we have witnessed in the first two chapters, the pulpit was for many generations a sacred space where only male bodies were welcomed, and still is in some traditions. The transgressing of that space in order to incarnate the gospel in a bodily way has not always been easy for women. For instance, many women of my acquaintance have had to suffer comments focused on their hair styles or their earrings after preaching their hearts out. A lesbian woman of my acquaintance was actually asked by someone on a pulpit search committee if she would consider changing her hairstyle and mode of dress to make her look less, well, lesbian. Women have had to pay far more attention to what they wear in the pulpit than their male counterparts. And a woman homiletician, Amy McCullough, wrote an article several years ago about the challenges of being a pregnant preacher and about the liberties so many parishioners felt they could take with patting and touching a clergywoman's body—liberties they never would have taken with a male preacher's body.[9] I still remember one of my early parishioners—an elderly

---

7. Karoline M. Lewis, *SHE: Five Keys to Unlock the Power of Women in Ministry* (Nashville: Abingdon Press, 2016), xxv. Italics added for emphasis.

8. Lewis, *SHE*, 59.

9. Amy McCullough, "Preaching Pregnant: Insights into Embodiment in Preaching" (Academy of Homiletics Annual Papers, 2013), 269–80.

*Chapter Three*

woman in a small church in Virginia where I was serving right after graduation from seminary—taking me to task for even using the word *pregnant* in the pulpit. To her way of thinking, even language about birth and gestation and women's experience thereof had no place in the pulpit.

Yes, embodiment for women, and navigating its nuances while hanging onto to a woman's own sense of integrity and personhood, can be challenging. Yet the more women take their rightful places in the pulpits of our land, the more they express through their embodied proclamation the wonderful diversity of who God created us to be, the more they also open the paths for the diversity of those who follow in their footsteps to be their full selves as well.

Christine Smith's words rang true to me in my interview with her, when she said:

> I feel like, as time kind of marched on, I feel like women got more and more empowered and freed to truly bring . . . all of their women's self to the task of preaching. In the beginning we were weighing everything. We were weighing what we wore, we were weighing the language we used. . . . We were weighing everything. It felt like we had to. And it feels like as time wore on, women did not have to leave out parts of their humanity. . . . I think we still have to be careful. We're not in an ideal world. Women can't just do anything and have people continue to respect them. There are rules that women still play by in the institutional church . . . but I feel at least that we've had a voice in [making] some of the rules.[10]

## #4) Women's Voices as Normative Preaching Voices

When I was still a student in seminary some forty-plus years ago, a retired male homiletics professor had the opportunity to hear me preach one of my first sermons. After saying something perfunctory about the sermon in general (which I have long since forgotten), he went on to focus the majority of his comments on the nature of my voice (which I have never forgotten). "You have the same problem as my daughter when you

---

10. Christine Marie Smith (Professor of Preaching *Emerita* at United Theological Seminary of the Twin Cities), Zoom interview by the author, February 25, 2019.

preach." (His daughter was a seminary graduate and an ordained minister.) "Your voice is too high, so it is somewhat grating to hear. You need to learn to lower it, so that it is not putting off your listeners."

While I have certainly worked through the years to avoid letting nerves run away with my voice in the pulpit (which can, indeed, raise it to a higher register), I could not help but be struck by the fact that this was a *male* professor complaining about the "high" range of two *female* preaching voices—with no acknowledgment (or seemingly any consciousness) that he was doing so. The effects on me were nevertheless harmful, given that I was only just coming to believe that it was actually okay for me, as a woman, to preach at all. What I heard in his comments—even though this is not what he directly said—was that as a woman I would always have a major liability in preaching since I didn't have a deep, bass male preaching voice. That worry only added to my anxieties every time I got up to preach. I feared to open my mouth, certain that the "right" voice would not emerge.

That concern has also added to the anxiety of many women I have taught to preach through the years. Some of them, too, have a hard time imagining themselves fitting into the predominantly male models of preaching and preaching voices they have experienced in their lifetimes. They, too, subconsciously come to see their own voices as liabilities and so are sometimes hesitant to raise them to an audible level. They, too, struggle with viewing their voices as valid voices for preaching.

In her book *Women's Voices and the Practice of Preaching*, Nancy Lammers Gross helpfully distinguishes between two ways to talk about women's voices in preaching. One way is what Lammers Gross calls "Voice" with a capital *V*. Voice, in this instance, is metaphorical in nature, referring to the right of women to speak and articulate their perspectives as they interpret the Bible and the world through the lens of their own life experience.[11] I will discuss the claiming of this Voice and its effects on preaching more in the following sections as I discuss women's life

---

11. Nancy Lammers Gross, *Women's Voices and the Practice of Preaching* (Grand Rapids: Eerdmans, 2017), xix.

experiences and preaching, women interpreting biblical texts, and women theologizing in the pulpit.[12]

But what Lammers Gross makes focal for her work is the claiming by women of a second kind of voice in preaching: "voice" with a lowercase *v*, that is, "the literal, physical speaking voice."[13] For Lammers Gross, the use of voice is integrally related to women's embodiment. It is only as women come to love and accept their bodies that they can also come to love—and to assert—their full-bodied voices.

When I think about the varied women preachers and homileticians I interviewed in writing this book, as well as other women students and preachers I have listened to through the years, I think of the delightfully wide range of full-bodied voices I have heard in their proclamation. Some have preached in lower registers, and some in higher. Some have preached with great variations of emotion, others with less. Some have preached with more evenness of tone, others with wider variation. Yet what is consistently encouraging is how "normative" the *range* of those voices has become during the past fifty to sixty years—especially for those who hear women preach on a regular basis. Most congregants today know that there is no "one-size-fits-all" voice for women—any more than there is for men. And many actually delight in hearing the gospel proclaimed in far more varied tones and registers and rhythms than they did when the pulpit was populated only by men.

## #5) Women's Experience and Preaching

When I asked the foremothers of homiletics what the biggest changes were that women had brought to the pulpit, many of them commented—in one way or another—on the significance of bringing women's life experience into the pulpit.

Sr. Joan Delaplane responded in this way:

---

12. For a fuller discussion of the challenges women face in claiming their Voices (with a capital *V*), see Mary Donovan Turner and Mary Lin Hudson, *Saved from Silence: Finding Women's Voice in Preaching* (St. Louis: Chalice, 1999).

13. Lammers Gross, *Women's Voices and the Practice of Preaching*, xix.

What is significantly unique in a woman's preaching? I really haven't come to an answer to that except to know that the stereotypes . . . don't fit. To say that the woman's preaching is going to be more compassionate, more personal, more sensitive, I haven't found that necessarily. We have so many wonderful preaching men who are sensitive, and compassionate, and creative, and gifted.[14]

[H]owever, I think there is no question about the fact that men and women experience life differently. Therefore, when they approach the Word of God and they have their congregation in mind and experience where is God at work in our world, there is a difference. . . . I don't know that many men would find in the preaching experience a birthing metaphor, and yet it is [there] for me and it fits.[15]

Minerva Carcaño, the first Latina bishop in The United Methodist Church, responded in this way:

What difference have women in the pulpit made? I think it's made the witness more whole. I love to sit with a book written by a woman, a commentary on passages in Scripture, a book about the church, and hear the view of a woman. It's very different. . . . I think of those passages in the Old Testament of women being raped, of women being oppressed and dismissed. And to hear the voice of a woman who has had some of those experiences and articulates what it feels like as a woman. It is just so eye-opening. It feels like, "Yes, that's what I feel." And it just brings scripture to life. It brings a perspective that has been missing and that makes our life richer because it's now shared.[16]

She continued:

I think that is true in women's preaching as well. The stories of being out in the field and seeing the vineyard from the perspective of a woman who sets the table with those grapes and that wine is so different. And it's a contribution that we are less rich without.

---

14. Joan Delaplane interview, Part I.

15. Joan Delaplane interview, Part I.

16. Minerva G. Carcaño (Bishop of the California-Nevada Conference of The United Methodist Church), Zoom interview conducted by the author, December 6, 2018.

## Chapter Three

As I mentioned in the introduction, I grew up in the 1950s and 1960s hearing a lot of sermons preached by men—many of them very good sermons, I might add. They nearly all had a three-point framework, incorporated lots of interesting examples and illustrations, and held my attention even as a child. But in retrospect I also remember how filled they were with examples from the then-male world: sports stories, war stories, stories about cars, stories about fatherhood. It was not until I first started teaching my Women's Ways of Preaching course twenty-five years ago, and heard one of my students use the image of her grandmother quilting in her sermon, with the visual of a quilt spread on the Communion table as she spoke, or heard another student in that same class preach the first sermon I ever heard on the story of the banishment of Hagar and Ishmael, and another preach on the Hebrew midwives in Exodus 1, that I realized how starved I had been to hear sermons that lifted up and highlighted women's everyday experience. Many of us have by now come to take such sermons for granted. And certainly during recent decades traditional gender roles have also changed and morphed so that many of the gender stereotypes that once frequented pulpits thankfully no longer fit. Our daughters or granddaughters these days would be just as likely to illustrate a sermon with a sports story as our sons or grandsons.

But what we need to remember is that such was not always the case. And one of the ways that preaching women have revolutionized the pulpit is that they have claimed it as a space in which to interpret scripture and theology and life from the vantage point of their unique experiences and perspectives on life. As Minerva Carcaño rightly observed, "That has made preaching and its witness more whole."[17]

## #6) Reclamation of Biblical Texts and Topics Not Previously Preached

Barbara Lundblad, professor *emerita* of preaching at Union Seminary in New York City and a former Lyman Beecher lecturer, remembers sitting in Marquand chapel at Yale Divinity School in 1982 when Phyllis Trible, a

---
17. Minerva Carcaño interview.

feminist scholar of the Hebrew scriptures, gave the Beecher lectures. Trible was the first woman to give the full set of these lectures.[18] These were the lectures that became Trible's well-known and now classic book *Texts of Terror: Literary-Feminist Readings of Biblical Narratives*. But significantly the subtitle Trible gave her lectures at the time was "Unpreached Stories of Faith." Lundblad recalls, "When she [Trible] talked about the dismembered woman in Judges, that her body was broken and given to many, and she lifted up the exact eucharistic words, you could have heard a pin drop in that chapel."[19]

Lundblad continues: "I love the kind of work [Trible] does with texts, and that there are women who have really not only been deconstructive of texts, but of looking at texts in such detail that it's been a different way of interpreting scripture.... Women scripture scholars have just opened up texts in a way that just wasn't true for many, many years.'"[20]

Mary Catherine Hilkert, professor of theology at Notre Dame and another former Beecher lecturer, echoed similar sentiments. When I asked her about the difference women preaching have made she said:

> I think central would be biblical hermeneutics, the feminist biblical scholarship.... I'm really delighted to find that male as well as female students are searching the feminist or womanist or mujerista or postcolonial or liberationist hermeneutical resources that are there for Bible scholars. I think we all know there's not one central commentary or one meaning of the text. And so I think that's been huge.[21]

Both Lundblad and Hilkert point to the fact that women preachers have not opened up new biblical texts on their own; they have been greatly assisted in that endeavor by the many outstanding feminist and womanist and mujerista biblical scholars who have given them new lenses for reading the story of Hagar, the story of the midwives Shiphrah and Puah, the

---

18. One laywoman, Helen Kenyon, had given one of seven lectures in 1950.

19. Barbara K. Lundblad (Joe R. Engle Professor of Homiletics *Emerita*, Union Theological Seminary, New York), Zoom interview by the author, November 1, 2018.

20. Barbara Lundblad interview.

21. Mary Catherine Hilkert, O. P. (Professor of Theology, University of Notre Dame), Zoom interview by the author, December 5, 2019.

story of Vashti and Esther, the story of the Canaanite woman with the flow of blood, and the texts of terror in the Hebrew scriptures that Phyllis Trible lifted up for us. Consequently, women have been encouraged and inspired to bring into the pulpit many texts—and many topics—they might not have preached on otherwise.

One of the assignments I have given my Women's Ways of Preaching class through the years is to preach a sermon on one of the texts of terror in the Hebrew scriptures. As a consequence I have heard incredibly moving sermons on rape, incest, domestic violence, genital mutilation, and the like. These sermons simply would not have been preached fifty or sixty years ago. And indeed, it takes a great deal of courage to preach them now. But by doing so, women—as well as courageous men—are opening up biblical texts that have long been ignored or glossed over by the church and have painfully named the experiences of misogyny and oppression all too many women have experienced, not only in biblical times, but today as well. As a result, the pulpit has become a more honest, more transparent, and yes, more challenging place to be. And our image of God has moved beyond sweetness and light to become the God whose body was broken with ours and whose blood was shed with ours.

## #7) A Safer Space in Which Women and Others Oppressed Can Hear Sermons

When I asked Barbara Lundblad about the harm she has seen done to women by the lack of women's ordination for so long in history, she responded in this way: "A friend of mine . . . someone I have come to know through church circles . . . said to me quite some years ago, 'I feel *safe* when I hear you preach.' I thought [at the time], this means she has not felt safe."[22]

Lundblad continued:

> Women have heard demeaning things said about women, almost just a tossaway line, a little illustration about a silly old woman, I mean, in a way that isn't usually said about a silly old man, just those kinds of diminishment

---

22. Barbara Lundblad interview.

and demeaning. And then downright dangerous. I think in terms of LGBT people, yes, terribly dangerous things have been said.

So women didn't hear their lives affirmed in any way. I think it's the harm of neglect, and it's also the harm of diminishment and demeaning that women have heard over the years.[23]

Some of my colleagues in teaching preaching could testify that over the years we have heard a number of students talk about the harm and diminishment and demeaning that has come to them through the church and its preaching. And when we put those realities within the larger context of the sexual misconduct and pedophilia and gender and sexuality shaming that has gone on in the church for decades in the name of God, it is no wonder that many women—and a number of men and transgender folk as well—no longer find it to be a "safe space" for them.

One of the things women have brought to the pulpit is the overturning of some of that diminishment and demeaning language. Some of it has come through the reinterpretation of biblical characters such as Hagar and Miriam and Mary Magdalene. Some of it has come through the positive images of women used in the stories told and examples women have woven into their sermons. Some of it has come through the exercise of a leadership style that invites and encourages congregational participation, not authoritarian acquiescence. And some of it has come from the sheer presence in the pulpit of a woman who also openly advocates for women.

I currently worship in a church whose senior pastor is a woman,[24] and I recently told her that one of the great gifts to me in worship is that I don't have to worry about something offensive being said or done. Rather I look forward to worship where women and men; gay, lesbian, and transgendered persons; and babies and teenagers are all welcomed and all invited into a space that is genuinely safe and encouraging and life-affirming. *Would that that were the case in the whole church of Christ.* I think that it is largely thanks to women's modeling, and men's growing

---

23. Barbara Lundblad interview.

24. I worship at First Presbyterian Church in Durham, North Carolina. Rev. Mindy Douglas (who was also my student three decades ago!) is my wonderful pastor.

Chapter Three

sensitivities to women's concerns, that church is becoming a safer space for us all.

## #8) Authority in Preaching Is Exercised in a Less Hierarchical, More Invitational Way

One of the questions I asked the women I interviewed was to reflect upon the way in which authority had been redefined for them in light of women's preaching. Alyce McKenzie, professor of homiletics at Perkins School of Theology, echoed the sentiments of a number of these foremothers when she said this:

> I think authority is morphing from, well, from top-down authority, to the *authority of authenticity*. I think that's what resonates with a lot of people in a postmodern era. They aren't so willing to [do something] 'just because I said so'—like the kind of parental homiletic. As I tell the students, the best way to be the real deal, the best way to appear to be the real deal is to be the real deal.[25]

McKenzie continued:

> Of course, classic discussions of the inner calling emphasize the church's call, and the bearing of fruits. I do think there's an authority that comes from preparation. I think that's extremely important. There's an authority that comes from that inward call. There's an authority that comes from the church's call. The way I look at it, we don't possess authority. *We participate in divine authority by being authentic.* Participating in a gift is different from claiming superior status.[26]

Lucy Rose was one of the original foremothers of the Academy of Homiletics, a person who ushered many of us early women scholars of preaching into its midst with an outstretched hand and a vibrant spirit. Lucy Rose lived a radically welcoming Christianity in the entirety of her life, and at the time of her all-too-early death to cancer, her household

---

25. Alyce M. McKenzie (George W. and Nell Ayers LeVan Professor of Preaching and Worship, Perkins School of Theology, Southern Methodist University), Zoom interview by the author, November 16, 2018.

26. Alyce McKenzie interview.

consisted of her spouse, Gerry, her young daughter, Lucy Mac, and two formerly homeless men, Dean and Louie, who lived with them as family. In her book *Sharing the Word: Preaching in the Roundtable Church,* Rose redefined authority in the pulpit in a highly postmodern manner. Rather than viewing authority in a hierarchical way—with the preacher being the ordained person sent by God who brings divine truths to bear in as persuasive a way as possible in preaching—Rose revisioned preaching as a *conversational event* in which the preacher brings to the congregation a tentative interpretation of scripture "that acknowledges, as best it can, its limitations and biases." The sermon's content, Rose writes, "is a *wager* on the part of the preacher: a new insight that has brought comfort or challenge . . . that is then submitted to the community of faith through the sermon for their answering meanings."[27] For Rose, the sermon was not the end of a process, but stood in the midst of a process of ongoing wrestling with biblical texts that began before the sermon was prepared—as small groups of laity met with the pastor to discuss the texts under consideration—and that continued into the future as congregants ruminated upon what they had heard in the sermon. Of critical importance to her in the process was actively summoning marginal voices in the congregation and hearing their perspectives on texts as well.

Margaret Moers Wenig is a Reform Jewish rabbi—the only Jewish rabbi, I might add, who attended meetings of the Academy of Homiletics for several decades. Wenig became interested in preaching because she felt it was the weak link in her own seminary training and so sought to expand her own knowledge of homiletics by regularly attending meetings of the preaching academy and interacting with other homileticians there. She also preached regularly at Beth Am congregation in Manhattan, while teaching preaching at Hebrew Union College–Jewish Institute of Religion in New York City. Rabbi Wenig reports that when she first became Beth Am's rabbi, they still had a tradition, going back twenty-five years, of gathering for an hour after their main worship service on Friday nights with coffee or tea and Entenmann's to discuss with the rabbi that night's

---

27. Lucy Atkinson Rose, *Sharing the Word: Preaching in the Roundtable Church* (Louisville: Westminster John Knox, 1997), 5.

sermon. She says that the feedback helped her immeasurably with her own preaching. She also invited four to six members of the congregation, generally those who disagreed with her, to offer their brief sermons or teachings during worship on Yom Kippur afternoon. And before she left for her first six-month sabbatical, she trained members of the congregation to read from the Torah, to lead worship, and to give sermons. That practice continued once a month after she returned.

Says Wenig:

> In Judaism one doesn't have to be ordained to give a sermon. My authority doesn't supersede the authority of my congregants, and my freedom in the pulpit comes from granting everybody else the same freedom. I never, ever, ever had to second guess what I was going to say. I never had to worry about what people's reactions might be because their reactions were welcomed, whether it was after the service or when they had the opportunity to speak from the pulpit themselves. That granted me freedom of the pulpit.[28]

Both Joan Delaplane and Mary Catherine Hilkert reminded us, when I interviewed them, of a key theological reason that Christian preachers, too, should be engaging in the kind of sharing of authority with the congregation that Wenig models. Namely, that for Christians, the ultimate authority for preaching is not granted through ordination but through *baptism*. "Our authority to preach," says Sr. Joan Delaplane, "is rooted in our baptism that we must share in word and in life, word and deed."[29] "Clericalism," says Mary Catherine Hilkert, "is a huge problem in all of our churches, and women in the Roman Catholic church do not exercise their gifts for preaching based on orders; it comes out of baptism and confirmation. It comes out of a call from the Spirit."[30]

One of the gifts women have brought to the pulpit is to challenge top-down notions of authority, and to redefine authority in a way that stresses both authenticity on the part of the preacher, and a more shared

---

28. Margaret Moers Wenig (Lecturer on Homiletics and Liturgy, Hebrew Union College-Jewish Institute of Religion, New York City), Zoom interview by the author, December 13, 2018.

29. Joan Delaplane interview, Part I.

30. Mary Catherine Hilkert interview.

and conversational style of preaching in relation to the congregation. As a consequence, preaching has become a far more communal endeavor than it used to be in the days when it was the congregation's task to remember and appropriate the three points of the sermon the pastor delivered to them.

## #9) Expanded Use of Narrative and Narrative Structures in Preaching

When I asked Jana Childers, professor of homiletics and speech communication at University of Redlands/San Francisco Theological Seminary, what changes she thought the presence of women in the academy and parish had brought to preaching she immediately responded:

> Well, we broke it open, didn't we? Or at least we were there at the moment to be a big part of breaking things open. Partly because of us the narrative movement [in preaching] got an extra push under its wings. There was so much affinity between women's experience and women's ways of thinking about the world in our generation as we were conditioned and acculturated. . . . So much match between our experience and worldview and the narrative movement. . . . Gene and Fred were before us, of course, but we extended things beautifully, in my opinion, through our use of story and bringing in women's ways of telling stories.[31]

The two male homileticians to whom Childers is referring are Eugene Lowry and Fred Craddock, who urged preachers to use more inductive and less deductive sermon structures as ways of engaging congregations, and who modeled in their work how to preach in ways that both literally used stories well (in Fred Craddock's case) and sought to structure a sermon like the narrative plot of a good novel (in Eugene Lowry's case). But the larger reality to which Childers points is that many women were also there cheering these two male homileticians on, because the way toward which they were pointing in their homiletical theory was also the way in

---

31. Jana Childers (Dean, University of Redlands Graduate School of Theology/San Francisco Theological Seminary; Professor of Homiletics and Speech Communication), Zoom interview by the author, November 26, 2018.

which women were naturally finding their own voices coming to expression in the pulpit.

Mary Lin Hudson of Memphis Theological Seminary echoed Childers's sentiments when she said, in relation to the changes women have brought to preaching:

> There's a lot more narrative, there seems to be more self-disclosure from the pulpit, a lot more dealing with the issues of inter-relatedness of people that comes . . . through women's attention to those human relationships and how important they are in relating the reality of God in community with each other.[32]
>
> I also think there is greater attention . . . to narrativity, telling the story, because I think women are much more sensitive to the fact that we live by different narratives, and the stories are what connect us in community with one another. By sharing those stories, we find identity and empowerment.[33]

I was reminded as Hudson spoke of how little personal self-disclosure there used to be in the pulpit by men of another era. Indeed, there was a whole generation of white males in the mid-twentieth century who were taught in seminaries never to talk about themselves in the pulpit, because doing so always distracted from their pointing toward God and God's word that had been entrusted to them. The theological assumption was that the word of God flows through the preacher, and that one of the preacher's jobs is to get completely out of the way so that God can speak without human interference.

Pam Durso, Executive Director of Baptist Women in Ministry, has published several volumes of women's sermons. When I asked her what, if anything, she found to be distinctive about the sermons in her collections, she commented on several things including the way in which women tend to be narrative preachers. But she also qualified that narrativity. "Women," she said, "tend to share personal stories that make them

---

32. Mary Lin Hudson (Professor of Homiletics and Liturgics and Associate Dean of Academic Assessment and Advising, Memphis Theological Seminary), Zoom interview by the author, December 6, 2018.

33. Mary Lin Hudson interview.

*vulnerable.* They then invite people to identify in the sermon with their own vulnerabilities."[34]

We have a far more embodied and incarnational sense of preaching these days, and in part it has come from the revival of narrative and personal storytelling in preaching that has made it a more humane and human act. Of course we always have to be on guard against preaching in which the story runs away with the sermon, or in which the personal sharing serves ends other than proclamation of the gospel. Narrative and personal storytelling can be used for ill as well as for good. But I would contend that the pulpit is a far more accessible and humane place these days because the gospel has been brought down to the ground of human experience, and the scriptures have been enfleshed in daily life in ways that allow people to glimpse God at work in their very midst. And women, and their storytelling, have played a critical role in that transformation.

## #10) Theologizing from a Woman's Point of View— about Everything

Preaching, of course, is a theological endeavor. We are always in preaching—whether we recognize it or not—shaping and reshaping theology as we reinterpret scripture and tradition and contemporary life and contexts in relation to one another. Thus, preaching by women is not only about bringing women's life experience into the pulpit; it is also about crafting theology through the lens of that experience and challenging theologies that do not lead to the liberation of all peoples—including women.

Once again, preaching women have been aided in this process by the many feminist and womanist, mujerista, and Native and Asian theologians who have gone before us and stood alongside us. These Beecher lectures (which have been revised for publication in this book) initially took place in a divinity school where the shadows cast by trailblazing theologians Letty Russell and Margaret Farley and Emilie Townes loom large, and where new visions of a theology that is more liberating for women and men alike have been birthed and nurtured. The church as a household of freedom in

---

34. Pam Durso (Executive Director of Baptist Women in Ministry), telephone conversation with the author, July 10, 2019.

which God is the householder/housekeeper (Russell), the ethics of a "just love" (Farley), womanist reinterpretations of evil and suffering and ethical responses (Townes)—these are among the many theological contributions by women that have shaped our preaching and influenced our thinking and led women to challenge oppressive theologies of the past even as they offer up new interpretations for the pulpit.

Certainly the cross has been a key place where women preachers and women theologians have been pressed to redefine traditional theology in ways that do not make God out to be some cosmic child abuser and Jesus some passive acceptor of the will of God. Scholars of preaching such as Sally Brown, in her book, *Cross Talk*, have joined forces with womanist scholars such as JoAnne Marie Terrell, in her book, *Power in the Blood? The Cross in the African American Experience*, to challenge traditional interpretations of the cross and Christ's suffering, while also evidencing the harm that those interpretations have done to women who have been told by the church to submit and sacrifice themselves—often to abusive partners—because that's what Jesus did and what God would have them do.

Christine Smith's seminal work, *Preaching as Weeping, Confession, and Resistance*: *Radical Responses to Radical Evil*, wrestles with how preaching can be a redemptive, and not an oppressive, activity in a world of radical evil. She writes:

> Part of our resistance to evil must be work *that is theological in nature and content*. Critiquing theologies of the cross that justify and condone human suffering of every description is an act of resistance. Suggesting that persons with disabilities know and experience God in ways able-bodied persons do not is an act of resistance. Participating in the redemptive work of breaking the silences surrounding rape, incest, and woman battering is an act of resistance. Preachers and communities participate in resisting evil as they critique and uproot theologies that undergird it and seek to build new theologies that bring embodied justice into the world.[35]

Women preachers and scholars of preaching have often led the way in breaking the silences, in reinterpreting the theologies that have oppressed,

---

35. Christine M. Smith, *Preaching as Weeping, Confession, and Resistance: Radical Responses to Radical Evil* (Louisville: Westminster John Knox, 1992), 9.

and in helping us see all people created in the image of God in ways that have challenged our cultural and traditional church norms. In the process they have also urged the church to *weep* with those who weep, to *confess* our own complicity in human oppression and suffering, and to *resist*—with all our beings—the forces of evil in our world.

Several of the homiletical foremothers I interviewed for this book commented on how significant feminist and womanist theology has been for shaping who they have become as preachers and scholars of preaching.

Mary Lin Hudson, the first woman professor at Memphis Theological Seminary, says, "Feminism, if anything, has taught me to look always for the subversive element in scripture and theology. That what the reality of Jesus does for us is it opens up the contradictions in our systems that seek to control reality. But God is bigger than that. And God is always in the process of subverting our certainties."[36]

Barbara Lundblad reflected upon the influence Letty Russell's theology has had upon her ministry and her preaching. "We've been celebrating this year [2018] . . . in Minnesota the twenty-fifth anniversary of the Reimagining Conference of 1993. . . . I think of Letty Russell, being one of my teachers at Yale, and how she just opened up a way meetings ought to run, or how people ought to get together and share leadership, rather than have one person at the top, and have a round table rather than a proscenium stage."[37]

For Gennifer Brooks, a feminist or womanist perspective in homiletics presses us to ask questions regarding what we're writing about. "We can't simply write about the things that concern women. We've got to write about everything. . . . To be in the middle of all the important issues, that for me is where we women have to make a difference . . . to put our feet in the middle of the mess and to speak out loudly and strongly, so that they can't avoid us. That I think is what is critical."[38]

If you survey the books written by women homileticians over the past thirty to forty years, you will find that women, indeed, have been writing

---

36. Mary Lin Hudson interview.
37. Barbara Lundblad interview.
38. Gennifer Brooks interview.

about everything. They have written about drama and performance in preaching, voice and preaching, and creative writing for preaching. They have written about biblical hermeneutics and preaching, theology and preaching, and the history of preaching. They have written about congregational contexts for preaching, how to preach through congregational resistance to change, and the process of birthing the sermon. They have written about wisdom preaching, prophetic preaching, and roundtable preaching. And they have written about preaching that is more sensitive to people with disabilities, preaching in Korean American cultures, preaching at weddings, and preaching to churches who fall in the purple zone.

Women have indeed "put their feet in the middle of the mess" and have theologized about how to preach for a wide variety of listeners in a wide variety of settings. And in the process, they have challenged, expanded, and transformed both *how* the field of homiletics thinks and *what* it thinks about.

## In Summary

When I asked Christine Smith, the author of the first homiletical treatise that provided a feminist perspective on preaching, how she saw the changes women had brought to the field of preaching, she responded in a way that also summarizes what I've been trying to say in this book as a whole:

> I do feel that women have revolutionized the church, I do. I have never said that (before). That's extremely optimistic, but I actually believe it. And I think, from everything from how we run a meeting, to how we preach, to what we do in worship, and the bigger way many of us understand worship, and just how we do pastoral care. I really think that people [parishioners] have been on the receiving end of . . . tons of change, and I don't even know if you ask people if they recognized key moments. I don't even know if they'd be able to say, but it just slowly and steadily and persistently, I think . . . has been a revolutionizing of a field, and of the practice of ministry.[39]

---

39. Christine Smith interview.

I heartily concur. In ways many of us could not even begin to name or identify or even recognize, clergywomen and other women in ministry have been revolutionizing the practice of preaching and other practices of ministry for a number of decades now. Women have revolutionized our understanding of who can speak for God and who has a right to claim the pulpit as sacred space. They have revolutionized the ways in which we understand and experience embodiment in preaching. They have revolutionized our expectations regarding "voice" in the pulpit—and in what tenor and cadences and from what vantage points pulpit speech can occur. Women have revolutionized how we experience and understand authority in the pulpit, moving preaching from a top-down model to that of a "roundtable" model in which authority is shared by all. They have revolutionized the topics and texts that are deemed worthy for preaching, and in the process they have brought into the pulpit topics and texts that were long considered taboo by male preachers. They have shared their stories, their life experiences, their vulnerabilities in the pulpit—and by so doing have made preaching a safer and kinder space for others who have had their own voices and life experiences marginalized or ignored.

It is not only women preachers, but also women scholars in preaching who have brought about this transformation: bringing to the fore the herstories of preaching women of prior generations (previously unknown and unheralded) for our edification and inspiration; publishing books related to the specific issues women face in preaching, and thus encouraging and mentoring women in their callings; publishing books of women's sermons, so that women are heard and recognized and their gifts celebrated by a broader audience; writing books that cover the waterfront of topics and concerns in the preaching field, so that women are no longer marginalized in the world of scholars, but are seen to be key participants in its present and future transformation.

These realities give witness to an astonishing amount of change that has taken place in homiletics in the past sixty years. And I would contend that both church and world are better for it.

Chapter Three

# Still a Long Way to Go

But if I'm going to end this book on a realistic note, I also must add: we still have a long way to go. There remain major challenges before us. *Ordained women are still very much in a minority in the worldwide church of Christ.* And there are major church bodies right here in our own country who do not yet ordain women or allow them to preach from the pulpits of our land. Those of us who believe deeply in the ordination of women need to offer women who still struggle to live out their own baptismal callings from God all the encouragement, support, and advocacy we can muster. As Minerva Carcaño put it, "We need to become midwives of what newness God is wanting to bring to the life of the institutional church."[40]

We also need to think creatively with women and other marginalized persons who are currently denied ordination or who prefer to preach from a non-ordained stance, and help them find places where they can live out their own baptismal callings to preach, rather than having to repress them. For when we deny people the right to live into their callings, we not only do irreparable harm to them; we also do irreparable harm to the church—keeping it from living into the fullness God intended for it and from imagining the fullness of the God who created us all—male and female—in God's image.

In a related way, we also have major work to do in *making inclusive language for God and humans the norm in worship.* I strongly believe this challenge is related to women's ordination because as long as we continue to use language that implies that God is male, we will also continue to believe—in some deeply subconscious ways—that women are lesser beings who do not deserve access to the pulpits in our land as fully as males do, and who are not fully created in God's image. Feminist theologian Mary Daly had it right almost five decades ago when she said, "If God is male, then male is God."[41] And yet in many of the pulpits and liturgies of our land, we continue to pray to God as if God is male, to talk about God as if God is male, and to use images for God that are primarily masculine

---

40. Minerva Carcaño interview.

41. Mary Daly, *Beyond God the Father: Toward a Philosophy of Women's Liberation* (Boston: Beacon, 1973).

in nature. What irreparable harm are we doing to our girls and young women (not to mention our boys) in the process?

I have long been drawn to theologian Sallie McFague's notion that the problem with our God language is the problem of idolatry. We have idolized Father language and male language for God and made them the norm, rather than using a diversity of metaphorical language to refer to our amazingly diverse God.[42] And in order to set the balance right, we need to call at least a partial moratorium on male language for God—not because Father language is never appropriate language for God, but because it is not the *only* appropriate language that can be used in relation to our God who defies the limitations of any one human metaphor.

I have to say that one of my deep sadnesses and frustrations in ministry is that during the forty years of my own ordination to ministry, I often feel that we have gone backward in terms of using inclusive language for God, rather than forward. I also believe the church's failure to embrace inclusive language is hurting the church's witness to younger generations—*especially younger generations of women*. I know women of my daughter's generation who simply will not worship in churches in which inclusive language and sensitivity to women's concerns are not the norm, and who consequently have a hard time finding places for worship that are life-giving for them. I hope and pray that as more and more clergywomen (and more sensitized men) take their places in the pulpits of this land, that we will see a reversal of this trend.

Finally, I want to say a word about *race and women's preaching*. One of the women who was the most forthright with me in my interviews with her about the role race plays in her vocation was Gennifer Benjamin Brooks. Brooks, Styberg professor of preaching at Garrett Evangelical Seminary, told me about recently being asked to write an endorsement for a new book in the field of preaching and of carving time out of her very busy schedule to do so—only to find that when the book was published, all the endorsements on the back of the book were from white homileticians, with hers omitted. Brooks rightly called the press not only

---

42. See Sallie McFague, *Metaphorical Theology: Models of God in Religious Language* (Philadelphia: Fortress, 1982).

to complain but also to tell them that she would never again write an endorsement for one of their books.⁴³

Brooks went on to tell me about other instances in which she felt that her race played a role—such as her difficulties in trying to recruit faculty for a DMin program in preaching she now heads, or of not feeling the same comradery with white women in the Academy of Homiletics that she feels with African American women, or of feeling that when she or one of her African American colleagues writes a book about preaching it is often pigeonholed as an African American resource and not a resource for the entire field of preaching.

I deeply appreciated Brooks's candor with me and her calling attention to the work we need to do within our field regarding race and how it affects our working relationships. Race is always a complicated and difficult topic to address. But I hope in the years to come, the field of homiletics will begin doing so in more systematic ways, so that clergywomen and scholars of color receive the support and affirmation they so rightly deserve. A good first step was taken by the Academy of Homiletics in 2019 when the theme for its annual meeting was "Unmasking Homiletical Whiteness."⁴⁴

## Conclusion

I want to end this book by paying tribute once again to Sr. Joan Delaplane, the first woman member and the first woman president of the North American Academy of Homiletics. When I interviewed Sr. Joan and asked her what final words she would like to say to me at the end of our interview, this is what she said:

> Of all times, I think our present day and age needs the preached word as never before. I think we've lost our moorings. . . . God is doing a new thing, and structures are coming down that have to come down in our nation and

---

43. Gennifer Brooks interview.

44. I am grateful to the 2019 Academy of Homiletics President, Sally A. Brown (Elizabeth M. Engle Associate Professor of Preaching and Worship, Princeton Theological Seminary), for selecting this theme for the annual meeting.

in our church. But in that process, we need to be rooted and grounded, and hear the word of hope and love, and that our evolutionary God is working in the midst of this mess.[45]

That good news is what we preachers of the gospel—whether we are ordained or lay, male or female, cisgender or transgender—are called to preach: a word of hope and love, the promise that our God is still working in the midst of this mess, and the vision of a day when all people of faith who have been called to preach will be able to exercise that charism freely, fully, and without censorship. Let us pray and work for that day together.

---

45. Joan Delaplane interview, Part I.

## Appendix A
# Homiletical Foremothers Interviewed for This Book

*In preparation for the 2019 Beecher lectures and for this book, I interviewed sixteen "foremothers" of the field of homiletics. Their brief bios are included below. This list is certainly not exhaustive; indeed, I regret that several significant foremothers from whom I requested interviews were not able to provide them. A list of the questions I asked the foremothers can be found in Appendix B.*

**Gennifer Benjamin Brooks** (UMC) – Ernest and Bernice Styberg Associate Professor of Preaching and Director of the Styberg Preaching Institute, Garrett Evangelical Seminary. Dr. Brooks is also Dean of the ACTS (Association of Chicago Theological Schools) Doctor of Ministry in Preaching Program. She is author of the following books: *Praise the Lord: Litanies, Prayers and Occasional Services*; *Unexpected Grace: Preaching Good News from Difficult Texts*, and *Bible Sisters: A Year of Devotions with the Women of the Bible*. She is also the editor of *Black United Methodists Preach!* She has served the Academy of Homiletics as a workgroup convener and is the first Black person elected to be the president of the North American Academy of Liturgy.

**Minerva G. Carcaño** (UMC) – Bishop of the California-Nevada Conference of the UMC. Minerva Carcaño is the first Latina to be ordained to the

Appendix A

episcopate in The United Methodist Church. She currently serves as Bishop of the California-Nevada Conference of the UMC (based in San Francisco) and previously served as Bishop of the Desert Southwest Conference (based in Phoenix) and the California-Pacific Conference (based in Los Angeles). She also served as Director of the Hispanic Studies Program and as adjunct faculty at Perkins School of Theology and holds an honorary doctorate from Claremont School of Theology. Bishop Carcaño is an outstanding preacher and a strong advocate for social justice. She is an internationally recognized immigrants-rights advocate and has long been an advocate for the full rights and inclusion of LGBTQIA+ persons.

**Jana Childers** (PCUSA) – Dean, University of Redlands Graduate School of Theology/San Francisco Theological Seminary; Professor of Homiletics and Speech Communication. Dr. Childers is the author or editor of eight books including *Performing the Word: Preaching as Theatre; Purposes of Preaching;* three volumes of the *Abingdon Women's Preaching Annual;* and the award-winning *Birthing the Sermon: Women Preachers and the Creative Process*. She has served the Academy of Homiletics in a number of capacities, including fourteen years as Treasurer and one year as President (2010–11).

**Linda Clader** (TEC) – Professor of Homiletics *Emerita,* Church Divinity School of the Pacific, where she taught from 1991 to 2013. She also served for ten years as Academic Dean at CDSP and was part of the core faculty for the doctoral program in homiletics at the Graduate Theological Union. Prior to teaching preaching, Prof. Clader taught Classics at Carleton College for nineteen years. She is the author of *Voicing the Vision: Imagination and Prophetic Preaching* and *Helen: The Evolution from Divine to Heroic in Greek Epic Tradition.*

**Joan Delaplane**, O.P. (RC) – Adrian Dominican Sister of the Order of Preachers. Of her almost fifty years of teaching, twenty-five were spent teaching homiletics at Aquinas Institute of Theology, now located in St. Louis, Missouri. Aquinas Institute is the only Roman Catholic graduate school of theology to offer a doctorate in preaching. The Delaplane Initiative for Preaching Excellence was endowed and named for her in 2013. Prof. Delaplane was the first woman to attend the Academy of Homiletics (the North American professional society for teachers and scholars of preaching), having joined in 1977, and was also the first woman and first Catholic president of that academy (1988). She retired from full-time teaching in 2002 and is currently a preacher, retreat director, and spiritual director, residing at her order's Motherhouse in Adrian, Michigan. She celebrated her seventieth year as a Dominican sister in 2019.

**Teresa Fry Brown** (AME) – Bandy Professor of Preaching, Candler School of Theology, Emory University. Dr. Fry Brown has taught at Candler since 1994 and in 2010 became the first African American woman to attain the rank of full professor. She served as Director of Candler's Black Church Studies program 2010–15. Her books include *God Don't Like Ugly: African American Women Handing on Spiritual Values*; *Weary Throats and New Songs: Black Women Proclaiming God's Word*; *Can a Sistah Get a Little Help: Advice and Encouragement for Black Women in Ministry*; *Delivering the Sermon: Voice, Body and Animation in Proclamation*; and *African American History and Devotions: Readings and Activities for Individuals, Families and Communities*. She is the Executive Director of Research and Scholarship, Fourteenth Historiographer and Editor of the *A.M.E. Review* for the African Methodist Episcopal Church.

**Mary Catherine Hilkert,** O.P. (RC) – Professor of Theology, University of Notre Dame. Dr. Hilkert gave the Lyman Beecher Lectures in 2010 and is currently finishing a book based on them, entitled *Words of Spirit and Life: Theology, Preaching and Spirituality*. She is also the author of *Naming Grace: Preaching and the Sacramental Imagination* and *Speaking with Authority: Catherine of Siena and the Voices of Women Today* and is coeditor of *The Praxis of the Reign of God: An Introduction to the Theology of Edward Schillebeeckx*. A former President of the Catholic Theological Society of America (2005–06), Dr. Hilkert has been awarded honorary doctorates from Providence College and from Aquinas Institute of Theology in St. Louis and Oblate School of Theology. A member of the Dominican Sisters of Peace (Order of Preachers), Sr. Hilkert has lectured and preached in Catholic and ecumenical contexts in the United States, Canada, Europe, Australia, and South Africa.

## Appendix A

**Lucy Lind Hogan** (TEC) – Hugh Latimer Elderdice Professor of Preaching and Worship, *Emerita,* Wesley Theological Seminary, Washington, DC. Dr. Hogan is the author of *Graceful Speech: An Invitation to Preaching* and coauthor of *Connecting with the Congregation: Rhetoric and the Art of Preaching* and *The Six Deadly Sins of Preaching: Becoming Responsible for the Faith We Proclaim.* She has served as President of the Academy of Homiletics (2014–16) and also as President of *Societas Homiletica* (2008–10), the international society of homiletical scholars. She was coeditor of two volumes of the international academy's papers: *Preaching as Picturing God in a Fragmented World* and *Preaching as a Language of Hope.*

**Mary Lin Hudson** (UCC; formerly CPC) – Professor of Homiletics and Liturgics and Associate Dean of Academic Assessment and Advising, Memphis Theological Seminary. Dr. Hudson has taught at MTS since 1988. She coauthored the book *Saved from Silence: Finding Women's Voice in Preaching* with Mary Donovan Turner. She also contributed the sections on Advent and Christmas to *New Proclamation: Year A in 2010.* Her doctoral dissertation focused on the preaching of Louisa Mariah Woosley, the first woman ordained in the Cumberland Presbyterian Church.

**Barbara K. Lundblad** (ELCA) – Joe R. Engle Professor of Homiletics, *Emerita*, Union Theological Seminary, New York, where she served from 1997 to 2014. She previously served as pastor of Our Saviour's Atonement Lutheran Church in New York City for sixteen years. Prof. Lundblad is the author of *Marking Time: Preaching Biblical Stories in Present Tense, Transforming the Stone: Preaching Through Resistance to Change,* and *Traveling on Holy Ground: Meeting Jesus Along the Way.* She has been awarded three honorary doctorates and received Yale's Alumna Award for Excellence in Theological Education in 2010. She is a former President of the Academy of Homiletics (2007).

**Alyce M. McKenzie** (UMC) – George W. and Nell Ayers LeVan Professor of Preaching and Worship, Perkins School of Theology, Southern Methodist University. In 2011, she was named as the Altshuler Distinguished Teaching Professor, SMU's highest teaching honor. Dr. McKenzie is also Director of the Perkins Center for Preaching Excellence at SMU. She is the author of nine books related to preaching including: *Preaching Proverbs: Wisdom for the Pulpit*; *Novel Preaching: Tips from Top Writers on Crafting Creative Sermons*; *The Parables for Today*; and *Making a Scene in the Pulpit: Vivid Preaching for Visual Listeners* (an expansion of her 2015 Lyman Beecher Lectures). She is a former president of the Academy of Homiletics (2012).

**Carol Norén** (UMC) – Wesley Nelson Professor of Preaching, *Emerita*, at North Park Theological Seminary. She previously taught preaching at Duke University Divinity School. Dr. Norén is author of *The Woman in the Pulpit* (1991), one of the first books to address the challenges faced by preaching women. She is also the author of *What Happens Sunday Morning: A Layperson's Guide to Worship* and *In Times of Crisis and Sorrow: A Minister's Manual Resource Guide*. She has particular research interests in Swedish Methodism in the US.

**Martha Simmons** (UCC; formerly National Baptist) – Creator and Director of the *African American Lectionary*, an online repository of resources for clergy and worship leaders and the only African American lectionary in history. She is also editor and President of the *African American Pulpit Journal*; editor of *Preaching on the Brink: The Future of Homiletic*; coeditor (with Frank Thomas) of *Preaching with Sacred Fire: An Anthology of African American Sermons, 1750 to the Present*, and coeditor (with Willie Francois III) of the *Christian Minister's Manual: For the Pulpit and Public Square for all Denominations*. Dr. Simmons has a passion for promoting African American preaching and women preachers. Since 2017, she has led a weekly Facebook Live broadcast titled "Preaching and Preachers."

**Christine Marie Smith** (UCC; formerly UMC) – Professor of Preaching *Emerita* at United Theological Seminary of the Twin Cities, where she taught for twenty-two years. She previously taught preaching at Princeton Theological Seminary. Dr. Smith is the author of the first feminist approach to preaching, *Weaving the Sermon: Preaching in a Feminist Perspective*, as well as of *Preaching as Weeping, Confession and Resistance*; *Preaching Justice: Ethnic and*

## Appendix A

*Cultural Perspectives*; and *Risking the Terror: Resurrection in This Life*. She is a former president of the Academy of Homiletics and was awarded a lifetime achievement award by that body in 2016.

**Mary Donovan Turner** (DOC) – Carl Patton Professor of Preaching, *Emerita*, Pacific School of Religion, where she taught for twenty-six years, and where she also served for six years as Vice President for Academic Affairs and Dean. She is coauthor, along with Mary Lin Hudson, of *Saved from Silence: Finding Women's Voice in Preaching*. In addition, she is the author of *The God We Seek*; *Old Testament Words: Reflections for Preaching*; *The Storyteller's Companion to the Bible, Prophets I, vol. 6*; plus many journal and reference articles. Dr. Turner is a 2019 recipient of the Lifetime Achievement Award from the Academy of Homiletics.

**Margaret Moers Wenig** (Jewish, Reform) – Lecturer on Homiletics and Liturgy, Hebrew Union College-Jewish Institute of Religion, New York City (1985–present), and Rabbi of Beth Am, the People's Temple, New York (1984–2000). Rabbi Wenig was an active member of the Academy of Homiletics from 1990 to 2016—the only Jewish member to participate regularly—and served as President of that body in early 2016. She has published numerous groundbreaking articles, and one of her sermons, "God Is a Woman and She Is Growing Older," has been republished many times nationally and internationally.

## Appendix B
# Homiletical Foremothers Interview Questions

1. When was the first time you heard a woman preach? What was the impact of that experience on you?

2. How did you come to recognize your own calling to preach? What were the particular challenges you faced as a woman sensing that call?

3. Was ordination to a ministry that included preaching an option for you? If yes, what challenges did you experience in the ordination process (both before and after ordination) because of your gender? If ordination to a preaching ministry has not been an option for you, how have you found opportunities to preach or exercise your vocation outside the channels afforded by ordination?

4. If you are a teacher/scholar in homiletics or a related field, what led you into this vocation? What obstacles or unexpected graces did you experience along the way?

5. For centuries, homiletics was a field that was almost completely dominated by men. Men had written most of the books and articles on preaching, taught preaching in most seminaries, were the stars of preaching videos, were the preachers most often heard on radio or television or depicted in movies. Ordination was not an option afforded most women.

## Appendix B

    a. What harm have you seen this history doing to women who have either directly or indirectly been denied access to the pulpit?

    b. What was it like for you as a woman to step into the "men's locker room" of preaching and/or its teaching? What gave you greatest joy in your vocation? What gave you greatest frustration and pain?

6. What did you find out about the use of authority in the pulpit and the nature of authority in the pulpit through your own preaching experience? About using a woman's voice in the pulpit? About your own approaches to biblical interpretation and theology versus traditional male interpretations? About your own approach to preaching in general?

7. What (if any) resistances did you experience to your teaching in the classroom because of your gender? To your scholarship and publications? What gave you greatest joy as a teacher of preaching (or a related field)?

8. What are some of the most significant ways in which you think the growing presence of women preachers and scholars has pressed faith communities to change their understandings of biblical hermeneutics, theology, ethics, and preaching ministry in general?

9. What do you hope your own most lasting contributions to the practice/study of preaching will be?

10. What do you see to be the biggest challenges regarding women and preaching that are facing us today? In what specific ways would you advise people of faith to advocate and press for needed changes?

## Appendix C

# Key Dates in the History of Women's Preaching and Ordination in the US*

## Seventeenth Century

*1634* – *Anne Marbury Hutchinson,* a Puritan, begins holding meetings at her home in the Massachusetts Bay Colony to study the Bible and review John Cotton's sermons. Around eighty men and women attend. Her opponents say she has "stept out of her place," call her an "American Jezebel," and banish her from the colony.[1]

*1640–60* – An estimated three hundred radical Puritan women prophetesses were active in England.[2]

---

\* Wikipedia provides a time line of women's ordination that appears to be largely accurate: https://en.wikipedia.org/wiki/Timeline_of_women%27s_ordination_in_the_United_States. I have taken that time line and have both edited and expanded it.

1. See Anna Carter Florence, *Preaching as Testimony* (Louisville and London: Westminster John Knox, 2007), 5–17.

2. See Curtis W. Freeman, ed., *A Company of Women Preachers: Baptist Prophetesses in Seventeenth-Century England: A Reader* (Baylor University Press: 2011), 17.

*Appendix C*

*1659 – Quaker Mary Dyer* is sentenced to death and is hung in Boston, Massachusetts Bay Colony, for defending her Quaker faith and the right of women to preach. Anne Hutchinson was a friend and mentor to her.

## Eighteenth Century

*1700–1775: Quaker women* (inspired by the Spirit) preach throughout the colonies and in Europe. As many as thirteen hundred to fifteen hundred women, ages seventeen to sixty-nine, preach on both sides of the Atlantic. In the US, they preach up and down the east coast, from Maine to South Carolina.[3]

*1740* – First Great Awakening in the USA. Personal conversion and regeneration become hallmarks of calling to preach. *Evangelical women* from various newer Christian denominations (Methodists, Millerites, Christian Connection) begin preaching as itinerants in the US. Catherine Brekus estimates over one hundred evangelical women (both Black and white) from these traditions were preaching from the mid-eighteenth to mid-nineteenth centuries in the US.[4]

*Mid 1700s* – Methodist movement gets underway in England, and women preach until Wesley's death in 1791, when the clamps come down. In 1787, the Manchester (England) Conference of Methodist Church authorized *Sarah Mallet* to be a preacher. In 1803, the men of Manchester Conference limited women's preaching to same-sex groups only.

*Late 1750s – Martha Stearns Marshall*, a Separatist Baptist, and her husband cofound a church in Abbott's Creek, North Carolina.

---

3. See Rebecca Larson, *Daughters of Light: Quaker Women Preaching and Prophesying in the Colonies and Abroad 1700–1775* (Chapel Hill and London: University of North Carolina Press, 1999).

4. See Catherine A. Brekus, *Strangers and Pilgrims: Female Preaching in America 1740–1845* (Chapel Hill and London: University of North Carolina Press, 1998).

Key Dates in the History of Women's Preaching and Ordination in the US*

# Nineteenth Century

*Second Great Awakening (first half of century).* Women such as Freewill Baptist *Sally Parsons*, Holiness Preacher *Phoebe Palmer*, AME preachers *Zilpha Elaw* and *Jarena Lee* preach as itinerants in the US.

*1815* – *Clarissa Danforth* is the first woman ordained in the Freewill Baptist denomination.

*1820s* – *Jarena Lee* is first woman licensed to preach in the African Methodist Episcopal Church by AME founder Bishop Richard Allen.

*1830s and 1840s* – Women's rights movement gets underway in US. Women such as Angelina Grimke, Lucretia Mott, and Elizabeth Cady Stanton claimed that women should have equal position to men in all of society.[5]

*Mid 1800s* – *Phoebe Palmer* has enormous influence as a Holiness preacher. Wrote *The Promise of the Father*, defending right of women to preach on biblical grounds.

*1853* – *Antoinette Brown Blackwell* is first Congregationalist woman ordained; had formal training in theology at Oberlin College. In 1863, she left the Congregationalist Church and became a Unitarian minister.

*1859* – *Catherine Booth* founds the Salvation Army in England with her husband; preached widely and argued for women's right to preach.

*1861* – *Mary A. Will* is first woman ordained in the Wesleyan Methodist Connection, which later became the Wesleyan Church.

---

5. See Beverly Zink-Sawyer, *From Preachers to Suffragists: Woman's Rights and Religious Conviction in the Lives of Three Nineteenth-Century American Clergywomen* (Louisville and London: Westminster John Knox, 2003).

## Appendix C

*1863 – Olympia Brown* is first Universalist woman ordained. Later became part-time minister in order to devote more time to the women's suffrage movement.

*1880 – Anna Howard Shaw (1847–1919)* is first woman ordained in the Methodist Protestant Church; was second female student in history of Boston University School of Theology, and also received a medical degree. She served two churches on Cape Cod; eventually left and became a prominent leader in the women's suffrage movement. Was greatly influenced by Quaker Susan B. Anthony.

*1880f.* – A network of twenty-one Unitarian women clergy begin preaching and forming churches in Iowa and on the American frontier. *Mary A. Safford* was a leader in this movement.

*1881 – Mary Baker Eddy* is ordained in the Church of Christ, Scientist, which she and others had helped form in 1879.

*1888* – African Methodist Episcopal Church officially decides that women can be evangelists.

*1888 – Clara Celestia Hale Babcock* is first woman ordained in the Christian Church.

*1888 – Frances Willard* reports in her book *Woman in the Pulpit* that 500 women are evangelists in the US in addition to 350 Quaker preachers and twenty women serving in congregations.[6]

*1889 – Louisa Woosley* is ordained by Nolin Presbytery of the Cumberland Presbyterian Church. Writes *Shall Woman Preach? Or the Question Answered* (published in 1891).

---

6. See Frances E. Willard, *Woman in the Pulpit*, Leopold Classic Library (Boston: D. Lothrop Co., 1888), 94.

## Key Dates in the History of Women's Preaching and Ordination in the US*

*1889* – *Ella Niswonger* is first woman ordained in the American United Brethren Church, which later merged with the United Methodist Church.

*Late 1880s* – First recordings of Northern Baptist women being ordained.

*1894 and 1890* – *Julia Foote* is ordained a deacon and then an elder in the AME Zion Church.

# Twentieth Century

*1914* – Assemblies of God denomination forms; ordains first women ministers.

*1944* – *Florence Li Tim Oi* becomes first Anglican woman ordained a priest (in China).

*1956* – United Presbyterian Church in the USA votes to ordain women as ministers. *Margaret Towner* is the first woman ordained. This denomination merged with the Presbyterian Church US in 1983 to form the Presbyterian Church (USA).

*1964* – Presbyterian Church US votes to ordain women. *Rachel Henderlite* is first woman ordained. This denomination merged with the United Presbyterian Church in 1983 to form the Presbyterian Church (USA).

*1964* – *Addie Davis* becomes first Southern Baptist woman to be ordained by a local congregation. The Southern Baptist Convention stopped ordaining women in 2000.

## Appendix C

*1970* – *Elizabeth Alvina Platz* is first woman ordained in Lutheran Church in America (which later became part of ELCA).

*1972* – *Sally Priesand* is first female rabbi ordained in Reform Judaism.

*1973* – *Emma Sommers Richards* is first Mennonite woman ordained.

*1974* – *Sandy Eisenberg Sasso* is first female rabbi to be ordained in Reconstructionist Judaism.

*1974* – *Katie Cannon* is first African American woman ordained by the United Presbyterian Church in the USA.

*1974* – *"The Philadelphia Eleven"* are "irregularly" ordained by two retired bishops in the Episcopal Church; their ordination is officially upheld in 1977.

*1977* – *Jacqueline Means* is first woman "regularly" ordained to the priesthood in the Episcopal Church.

*1977* – *Pauli Murray* is the first African American woman ordained a priest in the Episcopal Church.

*1979* – *Reformed Church in America* begins ordaining women as ministers.

*1980* – *Marjorie Matthews* is first woman bishop in The United Methodist Church.

*1981* – *Lynn Gottlieb* is first rabbi ordained in the Jewish Renewal movement.

*1984* – *Leontine Kelly* is first African American woman bishop in The United Methodist Church.

*1985* – *Amy Eilberg* is first woman ordained a rabbi in Conservative Judaism.

*Key Dates in the History of Women's Preaching and Ordination in the US\**

## Twenty-First Century

*2000* – *Vashti Murphy McKenzie* is first woman bishop in the African American Episcopal Church.

*2004* – *Minerva Carcaño* is first Latina Bishop in The United Methodist Church.

*2006* – *Katharine Jefferts Schori* is first woman Presiding Bishop of the Episcopal Church.

*2013* – *Elizabeth Eaton* is first woman bishop in the Evangelical Lutheran Church.

www.ingramcontent.com/pod-product-compliance
Lightning Source LLC
Chambersburg PA
CBHW011721220426
43664CB00023B/2902